# SELF-LOVE FOR WOMEN

## 10 Minutes a Day to Build Self-Worth Boost Confidence and Embrace Who You Are

### WHITNEY PRUDE
PharmD, BCPS, NBC-HWC

# TABLE OF CONTENTS

# INTRODUCTION

I would imagine since you're reading this book, you've had some moments of deep self-reflection about who you are and why you matter. You may have moments where you don't feel like you recognize the woman staring back at you in the mirror, or you might critique and criticize her to no end. You may have even taken a step further and wondered, do I even matter? Am I even valuable or worth anything to anyone? You may feel as though there is a deep void inside of yourself and you have no idea where it came from or how to make it go away. If you can relate to these scenarios and feelings, you're in the right place.

Self-love is deep and complex and is often difficult to fully understand. We might confuse it with self-care by getting our nails done or getting a massage, but self-love isn't physical, it's emotional. It's the deep inner connection we have with ourselves, addressing our feelings and emotions, showing up with support and compassion, and fighting for what we truly know we deserve as a valuable human being. It's about truly understanding and embracing who you are at your core. If you're struggling with these concepts, know that you're not alone. Many women wrestle with self-love at some point in their life, if not throughout their whole life.

I was always very confident in myself growing up, but for most of my life I had no idea that was different than self-worth or self-love. My first realization that I didn't know my worth was in the midst of some extreme challenges in my life. My parents divorced when I was 16 and my world crumbled, but that was just the start of the struggles that led to my realization.

I grew up in a very religious home and in a community where almost everyone in my entire city was my same religion. I loved my religion, I loved following the principles and standards that were taught, and I sincerely loved God and felt I had a very close relationship with him. I was a very focused and driven young woman. I enjoyed following the rules and I loved getting good grades and excelling in most things that I set my mind to, including academics and sports. My family praised me, my friends praised me, and my religious community praised me. You might see where I'm going with this, but I was very used to getting a lot of praise for doing all the right things.

When I was 21 years old, I served as a missionary for the church I grew up in. It was something I had dreamed of doing since I was a little girl. I lived in Norway for 18 months and I diligently shared the message I had grown up to wholeheartedly believe in. I spent every minute of every day serving others and growing closer to God. At the completion of the 18 months, I would have told you that I felt like I had touched heaven. When I returned home everything changed.

I was thrown back into reality. My family situation was still very challenging, and relationships were fragile. I was accepted to pharmacy school and the stress and overwhelm were incomprehensible. I was trying so hard to do all the right things, but I was crumbling. The closeness I felt to God was slowly dwindling and I had to dedicate all my time to studying pharmacy. By the end of my first year, I felt completely numb. I was a walking zombie, miserable and just trying to survive.

I needed God in my life at that time more than ever and I felt absolutely nothing. My feeling of "heaven" had completely disappeared. Through my despair I began to question everything. Was God even real? Did I make all of this up in my own head? Did anyone in my family really love me? What if I didn't believe in God anymore? What if I didn't stick with my religion? Could I still be loved? I was ashamed, confused, and scared.

This was the moment in my life when I realized my self-worth was built on action. If I could do enough, accomplish enough, and do the right things I could be loved. When I began to feel detached from everything I once knew and found comfort in, I felt completely and utterly hopeless. I had no idea who I was. I didn't know how to show up for myself and I certainly didn't understand my own self-worth.

This is where my journey to self-love began, and I am excited to share everything that I have learned with you. The purpose of this book is to guide you through the essential process of building a strong foundation of self-love, just like I did. It is designed to help you shed layers of doubt, embrace who you truly are, and step confidently toward achieving your personal goals. This isn't just a book; it's a transformative experience meant to help you cultivate a loving and nurturing relationship with yourself.

This book is structured to guide you through understanding what self-love truly means and why it is crucial. From laying down foundational principles to exploring advanced strategies and practices, each chapter builds upon the last. You'll find actionable steps and exercises designed to engage you directly with the content, encouraging introspection and personal discovery.

As a Board Certified Clinical Pharmacist and Certified Health, Nutrition, and Wellness Coach, my approach combines scientific understanding with holistic wellness practices. This ensures a comprehensive path to self-love that addresses your physical, emotional, and mental health.

To the women reading this, know that this book speaks directly to the challenges and aspirations unique to your experiences. Crafted with empathy and understanding, it aims to resonate with those seeking not only to enhance their self-perception but to truly transform their relationship with themselves.

As we embark on this journey together, expect it to be one of profound transformation. By the final page, you will not only have a deeper understanding of self-love but also be equipped with practical tools and strategies to nurture this loving relationship with yourself every day.

So, I invite you to join me with an open heart and mind. Commit to this journey not just as a reader, but as an active participant ready to explore, grow, and transform. It isn't going to be easy, but I promise it is worth it. Let's embark on this beautiful journey of self-love together, embracing each step with courage and anticipation for the rewarding path ahead.

# CHAPTER 1

# LAYING THE FOUNDATION OF SELF-LOVE

*"And you? When will you begin that*
*long journey into yourself?"*
– Rumi

Did you know that loving yourself is often overlooked in our journey to wellness, yet it's arguably the most important part? In a world that often encourages self-criticism and comparison, learning to truly love ourselves can feel like a revolutionary act. This chapter aims to dispel myths about self-love, redefine its meaning, and show how having a strong foundation of self-love is crucial for a fulfilling life. By understanding what self-love involves, you can begin to overcome doubts and cultivate a compassionate relationship with yourself.

## 1.1 Defining Self-Love: Beyond the Common Misconceptions

Self-love is often misunderstood as narcissism or simply pampering oneself, but it goes much deeper. It's about deeply valuing your own well-being and happiness, especially your mental and emotional health. It means treating yourself with the same kindness, care, and encouragement you would give to a close friend. This includes recognizing your needs, forgiving yourself for mistakes, and establishing healthy boundaries.

Self-love is distinct from selfishness. Selfishness involves prioritizing one's own needs at the expense of others, whereas self-love promotes a balance where you honor both your well-being and that of those around you. Setting boundaries is a crucial aspect of self-love—it means recognizing and communicating your limits so you can maintain your own well-being without infringing on the rights of others. For example, it might mean declining extra work responsibilities when you're already overwhelmed or opting for a quiet evening alone instead of attending a social event when you're feeling emotionally drained.

The connection between self-love and mental health is clear. Research indicates that those who practice self-compassion tend to experience less stress and anxiety. They are also more capable of facing life's difficulties without feeling overwhelmed. This resilience comes from a perspective that sees setbacks as chances to learn and develop, rather than as indicators of failure.

To bring this to life, let's consider two scenarios. In the first scenario, someone lacking self-love might continuously overcommit themselves. They say yes to every work request, volunteer for every school event, and never turn down a social invitation—all to please others. This often results in burnout. Contrastingly, someone who practices self-love takes a different approach. They prioritize projects that align with their passions and may delegate or decline tasks that don't. They are aware of their energy limits and honor them, which leads to a more balanced and fulfilling lifestyle.

Finally, self-love serves as the cornerstone for personal growth. It empowers you to pursue your full potential and engage more deeply in relationships. When you recognize your inherent worth and prioritize self-value, you're more inclined to tackle challenges that resonate with your passions and make a significant impact in your community. This doesn't imply immunity to setbacks or self-doubt, but with a strong foundation of self-love, you are better equipped to navigate and overcome them.

*Reflective Exercise: Self-Love Assessment*

Take a moment to reflect on your current practices of self-love with this simple exercise. On a piece of paper, rate yourself from 1 to 10 on how well you think you're doing in the following areas:

1. Setting boundaries
2. Treating yourself kindly in thoughts and actions
3. Pursuing activities that genuinely align with your passions

This exercise isn't about judging yourself; it's about gaining awareness and establishing a starting point for enhancing your practice of self-love.

By understanding and nurturing self-love, you pave the way for a healthier, more balanced life. As we continue through this chapter, remember that every stride toward loving yourself more profoundly is a stride toward a happier, more fulfilled you.

# 1.2 The Psychological Impact of Self-Love on Daily Living

When we start to grasp and apply self-love, it permeates every facet of our lives, profoundly enriching our daily experiences. Consider the last time you encountered a daunting decision. Maybe it was weighing whether to accept a demanding job offer or contemplating ending a long-term relationship that no longer felt fulfilling. These choices go beyond mere analysis of facts; they require us to connect with our core values and boundaries, where self-love becomes pivotal. It bolsters our ability to make decisions by aligning our choices with what genuinely resonates with us.

Self-love nurtures a deeper grasp of personal values and boundaries, crucial for making decisions that respect our authentic selves. For example, imagine someone declining a lucrative job offer involving frequent travel, prioritizing stability and family time instead. This choice, based on a profound understanding of their priorities, likely brings greater personal fulfillment and fewer regrets. Psychological theories like Cognitive Dissonance Theory support this idea, suggesting that aligning our actions with our beliefs and values reduces psychological strain and enhances overall well-being.

Moreover, the advantages of self-love transcend individual benefits to enrich our relationships with others. When we hold ourselves in high regard, we naturally establish and uphold healthier boundaries, fostering more satisfying and harmonious interactions. This enables us to confidently decline unreasonable demands and assert our needs without guilt. For instance, a woman committed to self-love might feel empowered to negotiate a more flexible work schedule, improving her ability to balance work and personal life and thereby strengthening her relationships both at home and in the workplace.

Self-love practices like meditation, sufficient sleep, and balanced nutrition are essential for managing our body's response to stress. They contribute to lowering cortisol levels, the hormone associated with stress, which, when elevated, can contribute to various health problems such as anxiety and depression. Prioritizing self-care not only enhances our mental and emotional well-being but also supports our physical health. This holistic approach to self-love ensures that we are better prepared to cope with the demands of everyday life without being overwhelmed by stress.

Finally, the resilience that comes from a strong base of self-love is incredibly valuable. Psychological resilience enables us to bounce back from setbacks and adjust to changes more effectively, reducing the likelihood of mental health crises. This resilience is nurtured through ongoing self-love practices that strengthen our capacity to confront challenges with bravery and positivity.

Self-love also impacts our physical health. By honoring our body's requirements, we adopt healthier habits and decisions that support longevity and well-being. These aspects will be explored further in this book.

By incorporating self-love into our daily routines, we not only improve our own well-being but also foster positive contributions to our interactions and relationships. It becomes a foundational element for leading a harmonious, meaningful life, where every choice and interaction reflects a deep sense of self-respect and compassion.

## 1.3 The Psychology of Self-Esteem: How It Forms and Falters

Understanding self-esteem is akin to peeling layers of an onion, with each layer representing various influences and experiences shaping our self-perception. Renowned psychologists such as Abraham Maslow and Carl Rogers have developed foundational theories that aid in comprehending these layers. Maslow's hierarchy of needs, for example, places esteem needs just before self-actualization, underscoring their significance in personal growth. Meanwhile, Carl Rogers emphasized the importance of unconditional positive regard—accepting and respecting others without judgment—as crucial for fostering healthy self-esteem. These theories offer a framework to grasp the intricacies of self-esteem and its profound impact on our lives.

From a young age, our self-esteem development is significantly shaped by our environment. Parenting styles, in particular, play a crucial role. A nurturing environment where parents provide praise and recognize their child's efforts helps cultivate a positive self-image. Conversely, a critical or unsupportive environment can lead to feelings of inadequacy.

Similarly, early experiences in school can either bolster or diminish self-esteem. For instance, a child who receives encouragement and praise from teachers may develop a strong sense of self-worth, while another facing constant criticism may struggle with their self-esteem.

These formative experiences are pivotal as they lay the foundation for our self-image and shape our beliefs about our abilities and inherent worth.

Negative experiences, especially during critical developmental stages, can have a profound impact on self-esteem. Bullying and social exclusion, for example, are significant events that can drastically alter a person's self-perception. Experiencing bullying or being ostracized not only influences how individuals view themselves but also shapes their beliefs about how others perceive them. If not addressed, these experiences can lead to a persistent decline in self-esteem over time.

For instance, a woman who internalized negative messages from childhood bullying may avoid social interactions as an adult. This avoidance can hinder her from forming meaningful relationships and perpetuate feelings of isolation and low self-worth. Addressing and healing from such experiences are crucial steps toward rebuilding self-esteem and fostering healthier self-perceptions.

The role of cognitive processes in shaping self-esteem is crucial. Cognitive distortions, such as all-or-nothing thinking, overgeneralization, and catastrophizing, can significantly distort one's self-perception. These patterns of thought often lead to negative self-talk, reinforcing poor self-esteem. For example, after experiencing a setback at work, someone might think, "I always mess things up," or "I'm not good enough," rather than viewing the situation as a singular event or a chance to learn and grow.

To address these distortions, cognitive-behavioral strategies can be highly effective. These techniques involve identifying and challenging distorted thoughts and replacing them with more balanced and constructive ones. For instance, if the thought "I am a failure" arises, it can be challenged and restructured to something like, "I made a mistake this time, but I have succeeded in other instances." This approach helps individuals develop a more realistic and positive self-perception, ultimately supporting healthier self-esteem.

Below is a list of common cognitive distortions. As you read through them, make note of any that you feel apply to you. Recognizing these patterns of thinking can greatly enhance your self-awareness and empower you to work on changing them.

1. **Not trusting your instincts:** Doubting yourself, overthinking, and letting others decide for you under the assumption they know better.

2. **People-pleasing:** Seeking approval from others, neglecting your own needs to satisfy others.

3. **Hiding parts of yourself:** Sacrificing your interests and ambitions, keeping your feelings to yourself.

4. **Perfectionism:** Setting unreasonably high standards, feeling inadequate regardless of your achievements.

5. **Self-criticism and judgment:** Being harsh and critical towards yourself when you don't meet your own high expectations.

6. **Ignoring your needs:** Not acknowledging that your needs matter, neglecting self-care, and feeling undeserving of it.

7. **Burying your feelings:** Avoiding uncomfortable emotions by denying them, using substances like drugs or alcohol, or avoiding situations.

8. **Not aligning with your values:** Doing things to please others even when they conflict with your own beliefs and principles.

9. **Codependent relationships:** Focusing excessively on someone else's needs and problems while neglecting your own.

10. **Not asserting yourself:** Failing to communicate your needs, not setting or enforcing boundaries, and allowing others to take advantage of you.

Now that you know about these cognitive distortions, begin keeping a journal—either on paper or electronically—throughout the day. Note when these distortions occur. Are there specific situations that trigger them? How frequently do they happen? Choose one distortion to focus on changing. What's one step you can take to start shifting this pattern of thinking?

Exploring these aspects of self-esteem reveals its deep connection to our mental and emotional well-being. Recognizing the causes and signs of low self-esteem is the first step in fostering a healthier self-perception. It's important to understand that improving self-esteem starts with identifying its origins and actively changing how we view ourselves. This proactive approach not only boosts self-esteem but also enables us to lead more meaningful and genuine lives.

## 1.4 Myth-Busting: Dispelling Common Self-Love Misunderstandings

Let's discuss some common myths about self-love because knowing what self-love isn't is as important as understanding what it is. First, there's the perfection myth. Many believe that if you truly loved yourself, you'd be constantly happy and free from struggle. But here's the truth: self-love isn't about reaching a perfect or always happy state. It's about accepting your whole self, flaws and all. It's normal to have tough days, doubts, or make mistakes. These things don't lessen your worth or your journey toward self-love. They simply remind you of your humanity, and embracing this is crucial in loving yourself.

Imagine you're picking up a new skill, such as playing the guitar. At first, it's natural for things to be a bit rough. Strings might buzz, chords might not quite sound right, and it can feel frustrating. If you believe in the idea of perfection in self-love, this frustration could lead to self-criticism and doubt. But true self-love means seeing each mistake as part of learning, being kind to yourself, and valuing the journey of getting better. This change in perspective is crucial—it turns difficulties into chances to improve, rather than proof that you're not good enough.

Moving on to the independence myth—the belief that self-love entails not needing anyone else and shouldering everything alone. This notion is not only unrealistic but also unhealthy. Humans are inherently social beings, and our relationships with others greatly contribute to our well-being. Self-love involves understanding when to seek support and how to accept it without feeling inadequate or weak. It's about recognizing the resilience in vulnerability and the bravery it takes to admit, "I need help." For example, on a tough day, reaching out to a friend for a chat isn't a sign of weakness but a step towards nurturing your mental well-being. It's acknowledging that while you are capable, you don't have to face your challenges alone.

Then there's the productivity myth, which links your value to what you produce, how successful you are, or how busy you stay. This was my biggest downfall. In today's hustle culture, it's easy to fall into the trap of thinking that your worth rises with your productivity. However, self-love challenges this idea by affirming that your value is inherent and unconditional. You are valuable not because of what you accomplish or achieve, but simply because you exist. Consider the times when you're at rest, like watching a sunset or enjoying a leisurely morning in bed. These moments, free from productivity demands, are just as meaningful and have as much potential for happiness as your busiest days. If you struggle with this, start by scheduling 10 minutes of downtime in your day where you do absolutely nothing but sit with yourself. This will be incredibly uncomfortable at first, but you have to sit in discomfort to allow yourself to begin to change.

Lastly, let's address the universality myth—the mistaken belief that self-love is uniform for everyone. In reality, self-love is deeply personal and can differ greatly from person to person. Cultural, familial, and individual values all play significant roles in defining what self-love means to each of us. For one person, self-love might involve pursuing a demanding career and excelling in a competitive setting. For another, it could mean choosing a less traditional path that allows for more personal or creative fulfillment. Acknowledging and respecting these differences is essential, not only in how we treat ourselves but also in how we empathize with and support others in their own journeys of self-love.

By dispelling these myths, we pave the way to grasp and embrace a more genuine, supportive, and adaptable notion of self-love. It's about granting ourselves the kindness to accept imperfection, the bravery to seek help from others when necessary, and the insight to distinguish our intrinsic value from our accomplishments. Furthermore, it involves celebrating the distinct ways in which each of us navigates and encounters self-love. As you proceed, remember that self-love isn't a universal remedy but a personalized journey toward living more kindly with yourself.

## 1.5 The Scientific Backing of Self-Love Practices

The concept that our mental state can physically alter our brain might sound like something out of science fiction, but it's a well-documented scientific reality. Engaging in practices like meditation and mindfulness doesn't just improve our emotional well-being; it can also bring about physical changes in our brains. Studies in neuroplasticity have demonstrated that regular meditation increases the density of grey matter in brain regions linked to emotional regulation. Essentially, the more you practice mindfulness and meditation, the more adept your brain becomes at handling emotions, leading to better mental health and reduced stress responses. Think of your brain like a garden: just as a gardener nourishes plants with water and nutrients, mindfulness nourishes your brain with positive input, fostering growth and resilience.

Self-love not only impacts our neurological health but also extends to our immune systems. Research indicates that robust self-care practices, which are integral to self-love, can significantly enhance immune function. These practices may include prioritizing adequate sleep, maintaining a balanced diet, engaging in regular physical activity, and employing stress management techniques. For example, studies highlighted in Psychosomatic Medicine demonstrate that mindfulness meditation can improve our immune system's responsiveness to pathogens over time. In today's context, where our immune systems face ongoing challenges, nurturing your emotional and mental well-being through self-love can fortify your body's ability to fend off illnesses.

Engaging in activities that foster self-love, such as yoga or spending time in nature, can lead to significant hormonal changes that enhance our overall well-being. These practices can stimulate the production of hormones like oxytocin and serotonin, often referred to as the 'feel-good' hormones. Oxytocin promotes feelings of trust and bonding, which can reduce sensations of loneliness and isolation. Meanwhile, serotonin plays a crucial role in stabilizing mood, promoting feelings of well-being, and increasing happiness. This hormonal boost isn't just beneficial for immediate emotional uplift but also supports long-term mental health.

Finally, the impact of self-love on longevity and quality of life is profound. Research shows that individuals who regularly practice self-love tend to live longer, healthier lives. This is partly attributed to reduced stress and its effects on aging. Chronic stress can accelerate aging by shortening telomeres, the protective caps at the end of DNA strands. A study conducted at the University of California, San Francisco, found that participants who practiced mindfulness and meditation had higher levels of telomerase activity. Telomerase is an enzyme that helps maintain and lengthen telomeres, suggesting a slower aging process and potentially lowering the risk of age-related diseases.

In essence, the science behind self-love goes beyond emotional well-being; it's about cultivating a healthier, more resilient body. These practices aren't just quick fixes but profound tools for transformation that can greatly improve your quality of life. As we delve deeper into the many facets of self-love, remember that each step you take nurtures not only your emotional health but also supports your physical well-being, paving the way toward a longer and happier life. This interconnectedness between mind, body, and emotional well-being highlights the profound and transformative potential of self-love, making it a priceless asset in our lives.

# CHAPTER 2

# UNPACKING PERSONAL HISTORIES

*"Where we come from is who we are, but we*
*choose every day who we become."*
– Hillbilly Elegy

## 2.1 The Role of Environment and Past Trauma in Self-Perception

If we were to uncover the roots of our emotions and behaviors, we often find that our earliest experiences and environments have played a crucial role. It's like tending to a neglected garden—unsettling yet essential for growth. Exploring your past may feel daunting; revisiting moments that shaped your self-perception may be challenging. However, understanding these influences is the vital first step toward reclaiming self-love. It's about gaining awareness, which gives you the power to make positive changes. Remember, it's okay to take this journey at your own pace, allowing yourself time to breathe and process the emotions that surface. This exploration isn't just about discovery; it's about forging a path to healing.

The environments we grow up in—our homes, schools, and communities—and the type of parenting we receive profoundly shape our sense of self from a young age. Consider a child raised in a home where achievements are celebrated and failures are viewed as learning opportunities. This child is likely to develop a sense of competence and self-worth. In contrast, imagine a child who faces constant criticism and feels that nothing they do is good enough. Here, seeds of self-doubt and feelings of inadequacy take root. These early interactions leave lasting imprints on our self-perception and influence our beliefs about what we deserve in terms of love and respect, both from ourselves and others.

Although we may not realize it, physical and emotional neglect are traumatic and can create wounds that last well into adulthood. Trauma is regrettably widespread. It may result from explicit abuse or neglect, as well as subtler forms like emotional manipulation or persistent undermining. Research underscores its prevalence, with studies indicating that a substantial portion of the population will encounter some form of trauma in their lifetime. These experiences can distort our self-perception and cloud our inner narrative, often convincing us that we are somehow undeserving of love and happiness.

The effects of trauma can be deep-seated and disabling, influencing how we perceive ourselves and our role in society. For instance, someone who endured bullying might battle with social anxiety and low self-esteem, finding it difficult to believe they are likable or deserving of friendship. Another individual who experienced neglect might continually seek external validation to validate their self-worth. These experiences shape patterns of thought and behavior that can be difficult to overcome without deliberate effort and support.

Acknowledging and understanding the origins of these influences is not about placing blame; it's about gaining clarity. By identifying the sources of our wounds, we can begin to heal them. We can confront longstanding beliefs that we are inadequate, unworthy of happiness, or perpetually need to prove our worth. This journey isn't easy or quick, but it's one of the most empowering ways to rewrite the story of your life and to begin treating yourself with the kindness and compassion you deserve.

*Reflective Exercise: Understanding Your Roots*

Reflecting on your upbringing and early environments can reveal powerful insights into your current self-perception. Take a moment to consider the messages about self-worth and achievement that were communicated to you, whether verbally or non-verbally. Write these messages down and reflect on how they have shaped your beliefs about yourself today. This exercise isn't about passing judgment; it's about fostering understanding and connecting the dots from your past experiences to your present identity.

As you continue through this chapter of self-discovery, remember that your past doesn't have to define your future. With mindfulness and compassion, you can begin unraveling the threads of past traumas and skillfully weave them into a tapestry of self-love and acceptance. This process supports who you are today and empowers you to become the person you aspire to be tomorrow. Every step you take toward understanding and healing brings you closer to embracing your true self with kindness and resilience.

## 2.2 The ACE Test: Understanding Your Trauma Score

In 1985, Dr. Vincent Felitti, the head of Kaiser Permanente's innovative Department of Preventive Medicine in San Diego, CA, established an obesity clinic. The clinic was open to anyone looking to lose at least 30 pounds, though it primarily focused on individuals who were severely overweight, ranging from 100 to 600 pounds. Each year, over 50,000 people underwent screenings for early detection of diseases using advanced tests and medical equipment, making it the largest medical evaluation facility globally at that time.

Despite the initial success of Dr. Felitti's department, he faced a puzzling issue: over the past five years, more than half of the participants in his obesity clinic dropped out of the program. Upon closer examination of those who left, he discovered that these individuals were actually losing weight when they decided to quit. This sparked a mystery that would lead to a 25-year investigation involving researchers from the Centers for Disease Control and Prevention (CDC) and over 17,000 members of Kaiser Permanente's San Diego care program.

Dr. Felitti started interviewing hundreds of clients who had dropped out of his program. Initially, he struggled to uncover the reasons behind their decisions until he began asking specific questions: How much did you weigh when you were born? How much did you weigh when you started first grade? How much did you weigh when you entered high school? How much did you weigh when you became sexually active?

His breakthrough came when a woman, his first patient, responded, "Forty pounds." She went on to explain, "It was when I was four years old, with my father." This revelation marked the beginning of Dr. Felitti's exploration into the deeper, often hidden roots of his patients' struggles with weight and health.

After interviewing 286 patients, nearly all of them responded in similar ways. However, another crucial piece of the puzzle emerged during an interview with a woman who had been raped at 23. In the year following the attack, she shared with Felitti that she had gained 105 pounds. She explained, 'Being overweight makes me less noticeable, which is what I need right now.' He realized that for these individuals, being overweight wasn't a problem but a solution. For instance, the woman who had been raped felt invisible to men, and gaining weight made her feel safer. Similarly, a man who was bullied as a skinny kid found that being overweight prevented further harassment. Another woman, who was abused by her father at a young age, believed that her weight protected her from further harm. Losing weight for them meant increased anxiety, depression, and fear to unbearable levels.

Over time, these findings extended beyond just an obesity clinic. They started to shed light on why hundreds of millions of people worldwide turn to substances and behaviors like alcohol, marijuana, food, sex, tobacco, violence, work, methamphetamines, and extreme sports to cope with intense feelings of fear, anxiety, depression, and anger. This research culminated in one of the largest and most significant public health studies ever conducted.

Between 1995 and 1997, 17,421 individuals at Kaiser Permanente's Department of Preventive Medicine completed a survey. The survey included the top 10 most common adverse childhood experiences reported by Dr. Felitti's patients.

The study's findings were astonishing:

1. There was a clear connection between childhood trauma and later development of chronic diseases, mental illnesses, incarceration, and workplace issues like absenteeism.

2. Two-thirds of the adults surveyed had experienced one or more types of adverse childhood experiences. Among them, 87% had encountered two or more types, indicating that experiences like having an alcoholic father often coincided with physical or verbal abuse. Adverse childhood experiences were rarely isolated incidents.

3. The more adverse childhood experiences a person had, the greater their risk of medical, mental, and social problems in adulthood.

A scoring system was created to assign one point to each Adverse Childhood Experience (ACE). For instance, if someone endured verbal abuse and lived with both a mentally ill mother and an alcoholic father, their ACE score would be three. Compared to those with zero ACEs, individuals with four ACE categories faced significantly higher risks: they were 240% more likely to develop hepatitis, 390% more prone to chronic obstructive pulmonary disease (emphysema or chronic bronchitis), and had a 240% increased risk of contracting a sexually-transmitted disease. They were also twice as likely to smoke, 12 times more likely to attempt suicide, seven times more likely to struggle with alcoholism, and 10 times more likely to use injected street drugs. High ACE scores correlate with increased likelihoods of violence, multiple marriages, frequent broken bones, more prescriptions for drugs, higher rates of depression, autoimmune diseases, and increased absenteeism from work.

So, why does this matter when we're talking about self-love? These early experiences don't simply disappear over time; they leave lasting impressions on how we view ourselves and what kind of love and respect we believe we deserve, both from ourselves and from others. It's crucial to uncover the underlying causes of your challenges with self-love. Below are all the questions from the original study. Take a moment to review them and give yourself one point for each question that applies to your experiences.

1. Did a parent or another adult at home frequently swear at you, insult you, belittle you, or embarrass you? Or did they behave in a way that made you fear physical harm?

2. Did a parent or another adult at home often push, grab, slap, or throw things at you? Or have they ever hit you so hard that you had visible marks or injuries?

3. Did an adult or person at least 5 years older than you ever... Touch or fondle you or have you touch their body in a sexual way? or Attempt or actually have oral, anal, or vaginal intercourse with you?

4. Did you often feel that nobody in your family loved you or thought you were important? Or did your family not feel close or support each other?

5. Did you often feel that you didn't have enough to eat, had to wear dirty clothes, and had no one to protect you? Or were your parents too drunk or high to take care of you or get you medical help when you needed it?

6. Did your parents ever separate or divorce?

7. Did your mother or stepmother often get pushed, grabbed, slapped, or have something thrown at her? Or was she sometimes, often, or very often kicked, bitten, hit with a fist, or hit with something hard? Or was she ever threatened with a gun or knife?

8. Did you live with someone who had a drinking problem or was addicted to drugs?

9. Did anyone in your household suffer from depression or mental illness, or did anyone attempt suicide?

10. Did any household member go to prison?

Count how many 'yes' answers you have. This is your ACE score. It reveals the underlying reasons why you may struggle with feeling worthy of love.

Understanding your ACE score can be enlightening. A higher score indicates greater exposure to adverse conditions, which research links to increased risks such as obesity, alcoholism, depression, and chronic diseases. Interpreting your score isn't about labeling or predicting your future negatively; it's about acknowledging how your experiences have shaped you. For those with higher scores, it's important to recognize potential challenges like increased stress susceptibility, difficulty in forming healthy relationships, or a tendency towards self-criticism, all of which can impact self-love development.

These experiences can profoundly impact self-love. Trauma can distort how you see yourself, often instilling a belief that you are fundamentally flawed or undeserving of happiness and love. This can lead to harmful behaviors, such as unconsciously seeking situations that reinforce these negative beliefs. For instance, someone who faced frequent criticism as a child might develop perfectionistic tendencies, always striving to prove their worth but never feeling fulfilled. Another person might find themselves in unhealthy relationships because they believe they deserve such treatment.

If you have a high ACE score and it's affecting your self-love and overall well-being, seeking help from a mental health professional who specializes in trauma can be very helpful. Therapy offers a safe place to process these experiences and learn healthier ways to cope. Connecting with support groups where you can share and learn in a supportive environment is also beneficial. Later on, we'll discuss a program that can further assist you.

Your ACE score is a tool that can shed light on your journey toward healing. It helps explain why you may feel and act in certain ways, empowering you with insights to pursue healing and personal growth. As you read further, remember that each step you take to understand and address your past is a step toward cultivating a more loving and compassionate relationship with yourself.

## 2.3 Mapping Your History: Identifying Key Influences on Self-Worth

To truly love and care for yourself, it's important to embrace and accept all parts of who you are, including the experiences that have shaped you. This isn't just about recognizing your past; it's about valuing how every experience has helped shape the person you've become. Every event, relationship, and choice has contributed to your self-esteem and how you see yourself. One helpful way to explore this is by creating a 'Life Map'. This tool lets you visually chart important life events, identify patterns, and recognize key moments that have impacted how you feel about yourself.

Grab a pen and paper and draw a timeline of your life from birth to now. Mark major milestones along this line—both positive and negative. These could include times of transition like moving to a new city, significant achievements such as graduating from college, challenging periods such as health issues, or profound losses like the death of a loved one. Connecting these dots can often reveal how your reactions to these events shaped your feelings of self-worth and your beliefs about what you deserve in life.

As you map out these events, take time to reflect on the relationships that have influenced you. Consider the people who have impacted your self-perception. How did your parents, siblings, friends, or romantic partners shape the way you see yourself? For instance, a supportive family might have boosted your confidence, while a critical teacher could have caused you to doubt your abilities. Evaluating these relationships helps you recognize their impact, enabling you to either strengthen healthy bonds or address and heal from relationships that may have harmed your self-esteem.

Beyond relationships, certain pivotal life events can significantly impact our self-image. These are moments or periods that may have fundamentally changed your outlook on life or yourself. For example, overcoming a major illness might have strengthened your resilience, while losing a job might have triggered a reevaluation of your career path and self-worth. Understanding these key events is crucial, as they often act as catalysts for personal growth or change.

To deepen this exploration, here are some reflective questions and journal prompts to help you analyze how these histories affect your current self-perception:

1.  What is one event in your life that you view as a turning point? How did it affect your view of yourself?

2.  Who are the three people who have most positively influenced your self-worth? What specific qualities or actions contributed to this influence? Now, ask the same questions about those who may have negatively impacted your view of yourself.

3.  Are there any recurring themes or patterns in how you react to challenges? What might these responses say about your beliefs about yourself?

4.  Reflecting on a past relationship that hurt your self-esteem, what lessons have you learned that can help you build healthier relationships now?

5.  Looking at your Life Map, what are three instances where you showed resilience that you can draw strength from today?

Engaging with these prompts not only helps you understand your personal history better but also empowers you to start redefining your narrative with a more compassionate and comprehensive view of yourself. This process is not about dwelling on the past but about using insights to build a more loving and accepting relationship with yourself. As you continue to fill out your Life Map, remember that each experience, no matter how small it seems, contributes to the complex, beautiful mosaic of who you are. Embrace this exploration with kindness, and let it guide you towards a richer, more grounded sense of self-love.

## 2.4 Breaking the Cycle: From Awareness to Action

Recognizing harmful patterns in our behavior and thought processes is like turning on a light in a previously dark room. It can be startling, perhaps a little uncomfortable, but ultimately, it illuminates areas of our life that need attention. Many of these patterns have developed as coping mechanisms in response to past traumas or adverse experiences. They might manifest as self-sabotage, where you find yourself undermining your achievements, or as people-pleasing behaviors, where you continuously place others' needs above your own. Sometimes, these patterns appear as relentless perfectionism, where nothing you do ever feels "good enough."

Identifying these patterns is your first step. You might notice, for example, a tendency to withdraw from relationships at the first sign of intimacy, driven by an underlying fear of rejection rooted in early childhood experiences. Or perhaps you recognize a pattern of overreacting to minor setbacks, a habit that may have developed from an environment where there was little security or predictability. These behaviors are your psyche's way of trying to protect you, based on the blueprint it developed early in your life. But now, they may no longer serve you and might actually be keeping you from living a fuller, more satisfying life.

The next step is breaking these cycles, which requires both knowledge and action. Cognitive-behavioral techniques are particularly effective here. These involve observing your negative thought patterns, challenging their validity, and replacing them with more constructive thoughts. For instance, if you often think, "I am not good enough to be loved," you could challenge this by listing evidence that contradicts this belief, such as remembering times when you have been loved and appreciated.

Mindfulness practices also play a crucial role. By staying present and engaged in the moment, you can observe your thoughts and feelings without judgment, learning to gently redirect your mind whenever you drift into negative or unproductive patterns.

Taking responsibility for your healing is empowering. It means acknowledging that while your past may have shaped you, it does not have to define your future. This might involve seeking therapy to work through deep-seated issues or setting boundaries in relationships to protect your mental health. It's about making daily choices that align more closely with the person you aspire to be, rather than the patterns you've outgrown. It's not always comfortable—true growth rarely is. But if you're feeling uncomfortable, it likely means you're pushing the boundaries of your old limits, and that's where real change happens.

One inspiring example comes from a woman named Maria, who grew up in a household where she was constantly criticized. Her journey involved recognizing how this environment led her to develop a harsh and unyielding inner critic. Through coaching and personal effort, she learned to silence this inner critic and replace it with a kind and supportive voice. Today, Maria runs workshops helping others do the same, transforming her pain into a powerful tool for helping others.

As we wrap up this exploration of breaking negative cycles, remember that each step you take is a piece of the puzzle in understanding and loving yourself more deeply. These actions are not just about overcoming bad habits but are steps towards a richer, more connected life. They are about reclaiming your power to rewrite your story.

As you move forward, remember that every effort, every small change, contributes to a larger transformation. This chapter has set the groundwork for the next, where we will explore how healing from the past paves the way for a future where self-love and acceptance are central to your interactions and decisions. Let's continue to uncover the layers, knowing that each step, each revelation, brings you closer to the wholeness you deserve.

# CHAPTER 3

# HEALING FROM THE PAST

*"Healing doesn't mean the damage never existed. It means
the damage no longer controls our lives."*
– Akshay Dubey

Healing from the past is like opening an old, forgotten book, with each page telling a part of your story. It's not about staying stuck in these memories but about understanding them and changing the ones that no longer help you. As you embark on this journey of rediscovery, focus on being kind to yourself. It's about using past experiences to grow a future full of self-love.

## 3.1 Unpacking Emotional Baggage: A Guide to Self-Auditing

Think of self-auditing as a way to lighten the load on your heart and mind, freeing you from burdens you might not even know you're carrying. This involves exploring your emotional depths and uncovering the feelings and memories that have quietly influenced your reactions and relationships. It's about allowing yourself to recognize these hidden influences, understand them, and transform how you relate to them.

Begin your self-auditing process with journaling, a powerful tool for self-reflection. Here's a guided exercise to help you start:

1.  Find a quiet space where you won't be disturbed.

2.  Grab your journal and a pen.

3.  Write down your thoughts and feelings from the past week. Let everything flow naturally without editing or judging.

4.  As you write, notice any emotions that stand out, whether positive or negative. These are your clues.

Next, categorize these emotions. While it may seem clinical, it's incredibly grounding to see your feelings laid out clearly. Draw simple columns and label them with categories such as guilt, joy, fear, resentment, or regret. Place your noted emotions into these columns. This visual arrangement can be surprisingly powerful, revealing where your emotional energy is going.

The next step is acknowledgment, which is crucial and often the hardest part. Acknowledge each emotion and experience without judgment. This doesn't mean agreeing that the emotions are justified or correct but recognizing them as valid parts of your experience. For instance, you might write, "I acknowledge that I feel resentful towards my friend for canceling our plans, and I recognize this is a valid feeling."

Finally, let's unpack these emotions. This means understanding the triggers and roots of your feelings. Ask yourself, "What exactly about my friend canceling made me feel this way?" Maybe it triggered deeper fears of abandonment or not being valued. Once you identify these triggers, you can start developing coping strategies. If abandonment is a theme, you might work on affirmations that reinforce your worth or discuss your feelings in a therapy or coaching session.

Here is a simple set of reflection prompts to help you through this process:

- What emotion did I feel most strongly this week?
- What situation triggered this emotion?
- What does this emotion remind me of from my past?
- How can I respond to this trigger in a way that honors my feelings and supports my growth?

This methodical approach to unpacking your emotional baggage is more than just a healing exercise; it's a liberation. It frees you from the cycles of reaction that unconsciously dictate so much of your behavior, allowing you to choose how you respond to the world around you. As you move forward, remember that each piece of emotional baggage you unpack and sort through is not just about lightening your load—it's about paving the way for a deeper, more authentic connection with yourself, where self-love can thrive unencumbered by the past.

## 3.2 Re-parenting Yourself with Compassion

When we talk about re-parenting, it's about filling the gaps left from our upbringing. Imagine, for a moment, that as a child certain emotional and physical needs weren't met; perhaps emotional support was scarce, or achievements weren't celebrated. This neglect can create an internal void—a deep-seated feeling that something essential is missing. Often, without even realizing it, you might find yourself trying to fill this void through external validation: you might become a relentless overachiever, a chronic people-pleaser, or someone who constantly seeks approval from others. The essence of re-parenting is recognizing this void and learning to provide for yourself what you didn't receive enough of: comfort, assurance, recognition, and love.

Re-parenting means nurturing yourself in ways you might have missed during your childhood. It's about being the kind, supportive parent you needed back then. This isn't about blaming caregivers; it's about taking control of your emotional health now. It includes things like establishing routines that make you feel secure, creating safe spaces where you can express yourself freely, and practicing self-care to affirm your value.

One of the most powerful parts of re-parenting is cultivating a nurturing inner dialogue. Many of us carry internal voices that are critical or neglectful, often reflecting past experiences. Changing this internal conversation requires deliberate effort. Start by noticing when your inner voice becomes harsh or critical. Pause and ask yourself, "Would I speak to someone I care about this way?" If the answer is no, take a moment to rethink how you could phrase that internal criticism to be more supportive and compassionate. For instance, instead of thinking, "I can't do anything right," you might say, "I made a mistake, but I can learn from it."

To deepen this inner dialogue, use a powerful visualization technique where you mentally connect with your younger self. Close your eyes and imagine yourself as a child during a moment of vulnerability, fear, or sadness. As your adult self, enter into that scene. Ask your younger self gently, "What's troubling you? Why do you feel this way?" Listen to your younger self express their emotions. Your role now is to provide comfort and reassurance. Say, "I understand you're upset, and that's okay. I'm here for you now, and everything will be alright." Conclude this visualization by offering a comforting gesture, like imagining giving your younger self a hug. This practice can profoundly transform your inner dialogue, replacing old beliefs of inadequacy with ones of kindness and support.

This approach isn't limited to revisiting past memories. You can apply it in current situations when you feel overwhelmed or distressed. When emotions are intense, take a moment to step back and use this technique: recognize what you're feeling, acknowledge that these emotions are valid, and affirm to yourself that you possess the strength and support to manage the situation. This method strengthens a self-support system that is resilient, attentive, and profoundly caring.

As you reflect on these ideas and contemplate these methods, remember the crucial step of putting them into practice. It's common to understand self-help strategies intellectually without implementing them actively. I encourage you to go beyond reading and actually engage in these practices. Take a moment now to pause, take a few deep breaths, and connect with your inner child through a brief dialogue. This simple practice is fundamental for healing and personal growth. It nurtures a relationship with yourself rooted in unconditional support and love—a relationship that everyone, including you, deserves.

## 3.3 Forgiveness: Healing Self and Others

Forgiveness is like shedding a heavy weight you've been carrying unknowingly—it liberates you, inviting more love and peace into your life. In the realm of self-love, forgiveness is crucial as it frees you from the burdens of past hurts, allowing you to fully embrace the present and future. Whether forgiving yourself or others, it's about breaking emotional ties to situations that have hindered your progress, marking a significant step towards reclaiming emotional freedom.

Yet, the journey toward forgiveness is often obstructed by significant barriers like lingering anger, feelings of betrayal, or the misconception that forgiving means approving of hurtful actions. These emotions are natural, but they can trap you in a cycle of bitterness and resentment, undermining your capacity to fully love yourself and others. For example, if someone has betrayed your trust, you might hold onto anger as a justified defense mechanism. However, this anger consumes emotional energy that could otherwise be channeled into nurturing and self-healing.

Giving yourself grace is essential in this journey. Often, you must forgive yourself as much as you forgive others. This might involve recognizing that you did your best given the circumstances or pardoning yourself for actions taken out of pain or ignorance. It's about accepting your humanity and understanding that mistakes are integral to your growth and learning. Reflect on times when you've been overly critical of yourself, maybe for not handling a situation perfectly. Forgiving yourself in these moments means acknowledging that perfection is unattainable and that it's alright to learn along the way.

To practice forgiveness actively, begin by cultivating empathy for both yourself and others. Try to understand the situation from the other person's perspective or reflect on your mindset at the time, if you're forgiving yourself. This doesn't justify harmful actions but can aid in comprehending the context and finding peace.

Another effective strategy is to reshape the narrative surrounding the hurt. Instead of seeing it as a deliberate attempt to inflict pain, consider the complexities involved—maybe the person acted from unresolved issues or miscommunication played a role.

Engaging in meditative practices centered on forgiveness can be highly impactful. Allocate a few minutes daily to sit quietly, take deep breaths, and concentrate on your intention to let go of anger and extend forgiveness. Visualize the person involved or the specific event and envision either sending them a message of forgiveness or receiving one from them, as appropriate.

This practice can bring profound healing, not just emotionally but also physically. Research indicates that forgiveness is associated with better heart health, reduced stress levels, and enhanced mental well-being. These benefits highlight how forgiveness contributes directly to your overall health, boosting your capacity to love and care for yourself.

As you engage in these forgiveness practices, keep in mind that this journey is for your benefit. It's about liberating your heart from the weight of unresolved emotions and enabling yourself to progress with a lighter, more compassionate spirit. Embrace these acts of forgiveness as chances for deep personal growth and observe how they pave the way for love and happiness to flow more freely into your life.

## 3.4 Overcoming Past Relationship Trauma

Navigating the aftermath of past relationship trauma can feel like navigating a field littered with hidden traps—each step can unexpectedly trigger old fears and insecurities. Your first step towards healing is recognizing the signs of this trauma. You might notice difficulties in trusting new partners or a tendency to withdraw from intimacy. Perhaps you find yourself stuck in unhealthy relationship patterns despite wanting something different. These behaviors aren't random; they signal deeper wounds that require your attention and compassion.

Relationship trauma can deeply affect self-love, causing significant and lasting impacts. It can chip away at your self-esteem, causing doubts about your worth and abilities in love. This erosion often shapes the kinds of relationships you feel you deserve, sometimes drawing you back into environments that mirror past pains—simply because they feel familiar. This cycle can tragically perpetuate itself, reinforcing hurtful beliefs about love and self-worth.

Therefore, healing from past relationship trauma is not only vital for your future relationships but also essential for restoring your self-love.

Understanding the dynamics of unhealthy relationships is crucial. A therapist once taught me a powerful analogy: the idea that 1/2 times 1/2 doesn't equal one, but rather 1/4. This means two individuals who haven't addressed their personal issues can't magically create a healthy whole just by being together. Instead, their unresolved issues can intensify, resulting in a less fulfilling and potentially toxic relationship. It's a stark reminder that personal healing isn't just a gift to yourself but also to your future partners.

Healing from relationship trauma is truly a journey, akin to any significant expedition—it demands preparation, guidance, and perseverance. Therapy and coaching can be an invaluable resource in this process, offering a structured environment to explore your emotional baggage and unravel your patterns. Support groups also play a vital role, connecting you with others who empathize with your experience, offering both insights and compassion from individuals on similar paths. These resources can provide crucial support as you navigate the complexities of healing and growth.

In addition to therapy and support groups, integrating self-care practices into your daily routine can greatly support your healing journey. Mindfulness exercises, regular physical activity, and engaging in activities that bring you joy all contribute to reinforcing your self-worth and building resilience for healthier relationships.

Here's an exercise I often suggest: Write down the qualities you desire in a relationship and reflect on how you can embody those qualities yourself. For instance, if you value understanding and patience in a partner, consider how you can cultivate these traits in your own behavior and interactions. This exercise encourages self-reflection and personal growth, paving the way for more fulfilling connections in the future.

Moving forward and cultivating healthier relationships after trauma involves prioritizing communication, boundaries, and self-awareness. It's essential to articulate your needs and emotions clearly within your relationships and to actively listen when others do the same.

Establishing and honoring boundaries is equally crucial; it safeguards your emotional well-being and promotes relationships that are respectful and nurturing for both parties.

Always remember, your feelings are valid—they represent your emotional truth. Recognizing and addressing them fosters transparency with others and is a significant act of self-love and self-respect. These practices lay the foundation for building relationships that are supportive, fulfilling, and based on mutual understanding.

As you journey through these experiences, continually affirm your strength and resilience. Every step you take towards healing and every pattern you overcome brings new opportunities for love and happiness into your life. Trust in your capacity to transcend past hurts and create a future where your relationships are shaped by the love and respect you have for yourself and others. Embrace the journey of growth and transformation, knowing that each effort you make moves you closer to a life defined not by trauma, but by healing and genuine connection.

## 3.5 Healing from Internalized Negativity

Exploring the landscapes of our minds reveals how profoundly our past, the words we've heard, and the treatment we've experienced shape our self-beliefs. The brain, with its remarkable capacity to create millions of neuronal connections, forms pathways based on these repeated experiences. Think of each recurring negative comment or toxic interaction as a raindrop on dirt, gradually carving deep grooves over time. These grooves, known as neural pathways, often become our default ways of thinking about ourselves, leading to internalized negativity.

Yet, the beauty of our brains lies in their plasticity—their ability to forge new, healthier pathways. This means that with effort and practice, we can reshape our thinking patterns, fostering positive self-beliefs and embracing healthier perspectives on ourselves and our relationships.

You may identify sources of internalized negativity in critical parents who expected perfection or in toxic relationships characterized by emotional manipulation. Narcissists, for instance, can profoundly affect our self-image. They employ tactics like gaslighting, where they undermine your reality, or give backhanded compliments that appear positive but leave you feeling inadequate.

Recognizing these sources is the initial step in comprehending how these experiences have shaped your self-perception. This awareness is crucial for reclaiming control over your self-beliefs and fostering healthier relationships with yourself and others.

To change these negative thought patterns, start by recognizing the negative beliefs you have about yourself. This isn't about accepting them as true, but simply acknowledging that they exist. Here's a practical exercise you can try now: make a list of the negative beliefs you often think about. Next to each one, write a positive belief that contradicts it. For instance, if you often think, "I'm not good enough," write down, "I am worthy just as I am."

Now, the goal is to reinforce these new, positive thoughts through repetition. Whenever a negative thought comes up, actively replace it with its positive counterpart. It's important to do this consistently; the brain needs repetition to change. Commit to practicing this daily. Think of it like exercising your mind—just as you would work out your muscles at the gym, you're training your brain to adopt a more positive and compassionate inner dialogue.

When negativity feels overpowering and you start to spiral, it can be beneficial to focus on positive distractions. These are activities that bring you joy and lift your spirits, like hobbies you enjoy, exercise, or volunteering. Engaging in these activities not only helps to divert you from harmful self-criticism but also boosts your self-esteem and reminds you of your strengths and value. It's important to remember that while these distractions are helpful, they are just one part of a larger strategy to reshape your thinking towards more positive and self-affirming thoughts.

By consistently using these methods, you'll start to see a change not only in your self-perception but also in your emotional state. Rewiring your brain requires persistence and patience, but the outcome—a more compassionate and positive self-image—is highly rewarding. With continued practice, you may find that what initially needed conscious effort becomes more automatic, indicating that new positive pathways are forming. This allows you to see yourself with greater kindness and authenticity.

## 3.6 The Truth About Sexual Abuse and Sexual Trauma

Sexual abuse and sexual trauma are sadly widespread issues that deeply affect the self-esteem of many people. It's crucial to discuss this here, not only due to its prevalence but also because of its profound impact on self-love and self-worth. Recognizing what qualifies as sexual abuse and trauma is the initial step in acknowledging its presence and beginning the journey toward healing.

Sexual abuse encompasses any non-consensual sexual activity forced upon someone, ranging from inappropriate touching to rape. Sexual trauma refers to the psychological effects these actions can have on a person. It's crucial to recognize that sexual abuse is alarmingly common; studies suggest about one in three women will experience some form of sexual violence in their lifetime. This statistic isn't just a number—it represents real individuals, possibly someone close to you or even yourself. Understanding that you're not alone can provide some solace in coping with such trauma and is a significant step toward healing.

When someone experiences sexual abuse, their brain's response can be profound. It often triggers a fight, flight, or freeze reaction, which is a basic survival mechanism. However, in cases of overwhelming threat, such as sexual abuse, the person may also experience dissociation—a disconnect between thoughts, identity, emotions, and memory. Even long after the abuse, the brain may continue to use these defense mechanisms in situations that subconsciously remind the survivor of the trauma. This can lead to symptoms like panic attacks, sudden unexplained fear, or emotional numbness in seemingly safe situations. Over time, these repeated stress responses can alter brain function, potentially causing chronic anxiety, depression, or PTSD.

I never expected most of the women that I would coach through my health and wellness program to have been sexually assaulted or abused in some way. They all came to me wanting to lose weight but discovered the root cause of their weight gain came from their past trauma. The problem is most women don't realize how damaging this can be for the rest of their lives if it is not properly addressed and processed. Take Mandy for example. She was raped when she was 17 years old. She was ashamed and began to isolate herself and withdraw from many aspects of her life. She never talked about it with anyone. About 10 years later she started a new job and was going through relationship challenges. She began having extreme panic attacks and mental breakdowns and was consistently having to leave work. She had no idea why all of this was happening. When she finally met with a psychiatrist she was diagnosed with PTSD from her sexual trauma. You can't sweep trauma under the rug. It will manifest itself in your life, it is just a matter of how and when.

Seeking professional help is crucial when dealing with sexual trauma. It's not something that heals on its own over time; it requires active intervention. Without proper treatment, the psychological wounds can persist, impacting both mental and physical health long-term. A trauma therapist possesses specialized knowledge in navigating these complex issues and can provide tailored strategies to help survivors regain control of their lives. Therapy may involve cognitive-behavioral techniques to change negative thought patterns, sessions focused on developing coping mechanisms for triggers, or group therapy where survivors can find support in a safe space to share their experiences.

If you or someone you know is silently suffering from past sexual trauma, please consider reaching out for help. Seeking assistance is a courageous act that signifies strength, not weakness. Recovery from sexual trauma isn't simply about returning to who you were before; it's about discovering the person you can become beyond the trauma's shadow. The journey to healing is undoubtedly tough, yet it's also marked by moments of significant growth and empowerment. Remember, regardless of your experiences, you deserve to feel safe, respected, and loved—by those around you and especially by yourself.

## 3.7 Dealing with Guilt and Shame

In the process of healing, guilt and shame often emerge as unwelcome shadows, stretching across our emotional landscapes. Especially prevalent after trauma, and notably in cases of sexual abuse, these emotions can deeply intertwine with our sense of self, making the path to self-compassion feel challenging. It's crucial to recognize and distinguish between these feelings. Guilt arises from regrettable actions, causing discomfort with "I did something bad," while shame is more pervasive, staining our entire self-perception with "I am bad."

Expressive writing can be a potent tool for untangling complex feelings like guilt and shame. It involves writing down your deepest thoughts and emotions on paper, not just as a record but as a way to release them. Here's how you can get started: Dedicate a few minutes each day to write about situations where you feel guilt or shame. Allow yourself to express everything openly, without holding back—let it flow in its raw and unedited form. Afterward, take a moment to read what you've written and reflect on the emotions you've expressed, without judging yourself. This practice can significantly reduce the emotional weight of guilt and shame by externalizing them, making them feel less overwhelming.

Practices of compassion provide another powerful method for healing, especially effective in addressing harsh self-judgments. Start with compassion meditation, a focused exercise where you cultivate feelings of warmth and care, beginning with yourself and extending them to others. Alternatively, try self-compassion exercises by affirming your humanity, inherent worth, and permission to make mistakes. Treat yourself with the same kindness you would offer to a close friend in distress. These practices aid in resetting your emotional responses, moving from self-criticism towards self-compassion and support.

Forgiveness, whether of others or oneself, plays a crucial role in easing feelings of guilt and shame. It involves releasing the grip that past actions have on your present self. Begin this process by identifying who you need to forgive—this might include yourself—and articulate the reasons why. Understand that forgiveness doesn't justify the harm caused but rather liberates you from its ongoing impact. If you're struggling with self-forgiveness, remind yourself that you did the best you could at that moment with the knowledge and resources available to you. Forgiveness isn't about forgetting; it's a choice to not let the past dictate your future emotional well-being.

Remember, no matter what has happened in your past, you are inherently deserving of love and respect. Guilt and shame do not define you—they are emotions that you can work through and evolve from. As you progress in processing these feelings, you'll notice their intensity diminish, creating room for more joy, peace, and authentic self-acceptance in your life.

As we conclude this exploration of healing from the past, we've delved into the burdens of guilt and shame, as well as transformative practices like re-parenting and forgiveness that lead us toward a more compassionate relationship with ourselves. Each step in this journey is a stride towards reclaiming your story, where you are the central figure deserving of compassion, understanding, and above all, love.

Moving into the next chapter, we will build upon these foundations, exploring how to cultivate resilience and turn your newfound insights into stepping stones for growth and empowerment. Hold these lessons close to your heart—they are the tools that will shape a life characterized by self-respect and deep inner peace.

# CHAPTER 4

# ESTABLISHING SELF-COMPASSION

*"If your compassion does not include yourself, it is incomplete."*
– Jack Kornfield

I magine standing before a mirror, not to critique yourself, but to genuinely offer kindness and encouragement to the person looking back at you. This might feel unfamiliar or awkward if you're accustomed to focusing on imperfections. But consider this: such a simple act could lead to profound personal growth and happiness. This chapter explores how transforming your inner critic into your strongest supporter through self-compassion can change your life.

## 4.1 The Path to Self-Kindness

Self-compassion isn't merely a nice concept; it's a potent practice supported by growing research highlighting its benefits for mental health and overall well-being. Dr. Kristen Neff, a leading researcher in this area, identifies three fundamental components of self-compassion essential for embracing this transformative practice: Self-Kindness, Common Humanity, and Mindfulness. These components, once understood and integrated, can deeply influence how you perceive yourself and cope with life's difficulties.

## Self-Kindness

Self-kindness involves showing warmth and understanding to ourselves when we suffer, fail, or feel inadequate, rather than ignoring our pain or harshly criticizing ourselves. It means recognizing that imperfection, mistakes, and life challenges are natural parts of being human.

Consider how you typically react when you encounter a setback. Do you tend to be overly critical and harsh toward yourself? Self-kindness encourages you to treat yourself with the same compassion and empathy you would offer to a close friend in a similar situation.

For example, instead of mentally beating yourself up for missing a work deadline, you might gently remind yourself that everyone has challenging days and that what matters most is how you proceed from here.

## Common Humanity

Common humanity involves acknowledging that suffering and personal inadequacy are part of the universal human experience—something we all encounter, rather than something that only happens to "me." This component encourages you to connect with others in your shared journey of life, rather than feeling isolated during tough times.

It's reassuring to recognize that you're not alone in facing challenges; everyone experiences difficulties and moments of feeling inadequate. This perspective can nurture greater emotional resilience and reduce feelings of loneliness.

For instance, if you perceive a failure, remind yourself that failure is a common experience shared by all, not a reflection of your individual shortcomings.

## *Mindfulness*

Mindfulness is a state of non-judgmental, receptive awareness where individuals observe their thoughts and emotions as they arise, without attempting to suppress or ignore them. Practicing mindfulness involves observing your pain or critical self-talk without becoming overly identified with these thoughts and feelings. This approach helps you avoid getting caught up in negative reactions.

Imagine a situation where you might feel intense anger or frustration. Instead of reacting impulsively or becoming overwhelmed by these emotions, mindfulness encourages you to acknowledge and observe them with curiosity and openness. This inner space allows you to consciously choose how you want to respond to these feelings, rather than letting them control your actions.

Embracing these three components of self-compassion isn't about denying your feelings or experiences but about changing how you respond to them. It's about saying to yourself, "I see you, I hear you, and I'm here for you." This nurturing approach can profoundly alter how you navigate life's challenges and joys, leading to a more balanced and fulfilling experience.

As we continue, we'll delve deeper into how you can cultivate these practices and weave them into your daily life. Remember, the journey toward self-compassion is ongoing—it's not about reaching a final destination but about making small, consistent choices that honor and support yourself. Let's take these steps together, with kindness and patience, as you learn to become your own best friend in a world that often encourages self-criticism.

## 4.2 Navigating Self-Kindness

Navigating through the labyrinth of your thoughts can often feel like finding your way through a dense forest without a map. It's easy to become lost, falling into pits of negative self-talk that seem to echo endlessly. The initial step toward forging a clear path is recognizing these patterns of thinking. It's about becoming aware of those moments when your inner dialogue shifts from being your own best supporter to becoming your harshest critic.

Negative self-talk often sets off a cycle of diminished self-esteem and heightened self-criticism, which can be deeply discouraging. We have discussed how to address these thoughts previously, but you'll notice how this practice can apply to many different aspects of this journey. To break this cycle, it's crucial to first pinpoint what these negative thoughts typically entail for you. Examples might include thoughts such as "I can't ever do anything right," "I always mess things up," "I don't know anything," or "I don't deserve happiness." Write these thoughts down throughout the day and then reframe each one to give you a resource of positive, affirmative thoughts you can repeat over and over. Here are some examples to help you know what to look for:

- I'm not good enough
- There's never enough time to take care of myself

- I might do it wrong
- I'm going to end up alone
- This shouldn't be happening to me
- Others are way more successful than I am
- I don't deserve any more in life than I already have
- I've never been successful, why is now any different?
- I'll never really change
- I'm just a failure, I'll never figure this out
- I don't deserve to be loved
- I'm stupid for feeling this way
- It's selfish to think of myself and my needs before others
- If I express my true thoughts and feelings others will reject me
- I'm so ugly, why do I even try to look good?

The next step is to reframe these thoughts. Instead of saying, "I'm not good enough," you might say, "I am a valuable human being and am good enough just the way I am." In place of telling yourself that others are way more successful than you, you might reframe this thought to say, "I have my own unique strengths and talents and can achieve whatever I put my mind to."

Identifying these patterns and working to reframe them is akin to recognizing the markers of a well-trodden path in our mental landscape—a path formed out of habit rather than conscious choice. In the next section, we'll delve deeper into strategies for navigating these thoughts and managing your inner critic effectively.

Mindfulness is also crucial in calming negative self-talk. It trains you to observe your thoughts and feelings without judgment, seeing them as passing clouds in the sky of your mind. Through mindfulness practice, you can cultivate the ability to step back from harmful thoughts and observe them with both compassion and objectivity.

Simple mindfulness exercises include fully focusing on routine activities like washing dishes, and paying attention to the sensations and movements involved. Another practice involves mindful breathing, where you concentrate on each inhale and exhale to anchor yourself in the present moment. Essentially, you are taking the time to pay attention to what is happening inside of you and around you in the moment. These exercises help you develop a greater awareness and resilience in managing negative self-talk.

By incorporating these practices into your daily routine, you begin to carve out a gentler path through your own mind—one where compassion triumphs over criticism and understanding displaces judgment. This transformation not only enhances your self-relationship but also enriches your overall quality of life. It empowers you to interact with the world from a foundation of self-respect and confidence.

As you persist in applying these techniques, remember that each forward movement, no matter how incremental, contributes to cultivating a more compassionate self with a kinder and more supportive inner dialogue.

## 4.3 Managing the Critic Within: Steps to Silence Self-Doubt

It's important to understand that this inner critic isn't an adversary but rather a misguided guardian attempting to shield you from pain and disillusionment using strategies it learned long ago. Acknowledging that this voice stems from past environments and experiences is the initial stride toward altering its impact on your life.

This is where understanding cognitive distortions becomes crucial once more. As a reminder, cognitive distortions are skewed ways of thinking that can exaggerate the negativity of reality. We explored the 10 most prevalent cognitive distortions in Chapter 3, so refer back to them if you need a refresher.

Engaging in a constructive dialogue with your inner critic and addressing these distortions is akin to negotiating with a skeptical friend who means well but is entrenched in their views. Start by acknowledging the critic's presence: listen to what it's saying without immediately trying to silence it. This approach may feel counterintuitive, but by listening, you gain insights into your deepest fears and insecurities.

Next, gently but firmly question its assertions. For instance, if your inner critic insists, "You'll never succeed," inquire, "Why do you think that? What evidence supports this belief?" Often, you'll discover that the critic's arguments are based on past experiences, not your current reality or abilities. Counter these arguments with reflections on your present capabilities and achievements, such as, "I have succeeded in similar situations before, and I have learned and grown since then."

Setting healthy boundaries with your self-criticism is essential. Start by identifying when this inner dialogue is constructive—it might motivate you to prepare well for important tasks—and when it turns harmful. If the criticism feels too harsh for someone you care about, it's probably too harsh for yourself as well. When you notice negative self-talk, imagine a stop sign to pause the flow of criticism. Then, intentionally shift your thoughts to more constructive and supportive ones.

Celebrating small victories is crucial for reshaping the impact of your inner critic. By recognizing and celebrating every success, even the smallest ones, you affirm your self-value and competence. These successes could be as simple as finishing a workout, delivering a successful presentation at work, or getting out of bed on tough mornings. Start a "success journal" where you can write down these wins each day. Over time, this journal will become a tangible reminder of your abilities and growth, reducing the power of your inner critic and boosting your confidence.

As you consistently apply these strategies, you'll observe changes not just in your self-talk but also in your self-perception. The inner critic, once a source of uncertainty, can evolve into a source of encouragement and insight, guiding you towards decisions that align with your true potential and value. Remember, this transformation takes time. It demands patience, persistence, and a generous dose of self-kindness. With each small step, you are developing a more nurturing and compassionate connection with yourself, paving the path to a life filled with confidence rather than overshadowed by uncertainty.

## 4.4 Embracing Vulnerability as Strength

Sharing our deepest fears, failures, and insecurities can feel daunting, like braving a storm without protection—exposed, uncertain, and profoundly vulnerable. Vulnerability often carries a stigma of weakness; we worry that revealing our true selves, imperfections and all, might invite rejection or criticism. However, in therapy, I learned a powerful lesson: genuine emotional well-being comes from aligning how others see us with how we see ourselves. This alignment hinges on embracing vulnerability. It means shedding masks and presenting our authentic selves to the world.

Redefining vulnerability as a strength rather than a weakness can transform how you relate to yourself and others. Embracing vulnerability allows for more genuine experiences and deeper connections. Authenticity attracts others because it reflects sincerity. It's about changing the perception of vulnerability from exposing weaknesses to embracing it as a chance to learn more about ourselves and cultivate meaningful relationships.

I've seen many personal journeys where embracing vulnerability has sparked profound growth. Consider Lisa's story: She had a passion for writing but hesitated to share her work, fearing criticism and self-doubt. When she finally took the leap to start a blog and share her thoughts openly, the response was overwhelmingly positive. Readers valued her honesty and openness, and Lisa gained newfound confidence in her abilities. Embracing vulnerability helped her unlock her potential and connect with a community that embraced her authentic voice.

Encouraging you to step beyond your comfort zone is essential when embracing vulnerability. It involves taking small, thoughtful risks that stretch your boundaries. For example, if discussing feelings or personal experiences feels uncomfortable, challenge yourself to gradually open up more in conversations. Similarly, if you tend to avoid expressing opinions, start by sharing your thoughts in relaxed settings like casual gatherings with friends then work your way up to speaking up at work. Each small step towards openness builds your confidence and comfort with vulnerability.

Embracing vulnerability offers profound benefits. It fosters personal growth, deepens self-understanding, and enriches relationships. When you are open and vulnerable, it encourages others to share their own truths, fostering empathy and meaningful connections. This creates a supportive community where genuine interactions thrive, leading to deeper relationships built on mutual understanding and support.

As you journey through life, reflect on how embracing vulnerability can reshape your interactions and relationships. Remember, vulnerability isn't a sign of weakness; it's a brave choice to welcome life's full range of experiences. By doing so, you cultivate deeper connections and lead a more authentic life. Embrace vulnerability not with apprehension, but with excitement for the depth and richness it can bring to both your personal growth and your relationships.

## 4.5 Self-Compassion Exercises for Daily Practice

### *Self-Compassion Breaks*

Imagine this scenario: In the midst of a hectic day, instead of turning to your phone or a quick coffee break, you opt for a self-compassion pause. You stop what you're doing, close your eyes, and gently place a hand over your heart—a gesture of warmth and care. Take a few deep breaths and acknowledge whatever emotions are present—whether it's stress, frustration, or fatigue—allowing yourself to feel them without judgment. Affirm to yourself, "This is a moment of difficulty, and it's okay. Difficult moments are a natural part of life." This recognition helps normalize your feelings and connects you with the shared human experience. By making these pauses a regular practice, you cultivate a gentler approach to managing life's challenges, reducing self-criticism along the way.

### Self-Compassion Mantra

Mantras are powerful tools to center and refocus our minds. Create a personal self-compassion mantra that you can repeat during tough times or when negative thoughts take over. Your mantra could be as simple as saying, "I am enough," or "Today, I choose kindness for myself." By repeating these words, you strengthen a positive, compassionate mindset that helps protect you from self-criticism. Use this mantra when you feel overwhelmed or self-critical—it's a reminder to treat yourself with the same kindness you would give to a loved one.

### Gratitude Journal

Gratitude helps us shift our attention from what we lack to what we have in abundance. Begin or end your day by writing down three things you're grateful for, especially focusing on qualities you value in yourself or accomplishments from the day. This might include recognizing your determination in a challenging project or acknowledging your kindness in assisting a colleague. Keeping a gratitude journal dedicated to these affirmations helps solidify them, gradually changing your inner dialogue from self-criticism to appreciation. This practice not only lifts your spirits but also strengthens your self-esteem over time.

### Loving-Kindness Meditation

Loving-kindness meditation is a practice that focuses on cultivating feelings of goodwill, kindness, and warmth towards oneself and others. Begin by sitting comfortably in a quiet place. Close your eyes and visualize yourself experiencing complete physical and emotional wellness, along with inner peace. Quietly repeat to yourself, "May I be happy, may I be safe, may I be healthy, may I live with ease." Once you've directed these wishes towards yourself, extend them outward to loved ones, acquaintances, and even those you find challenging. This meditation not only deepens self-compassion but also enhances empathy towards others, fostering stronger interpersonal connections.

Integrating self-compassion into your life is a gradual process. Our brains require time and regular practice to replace old habits of self-criticism with new patterns of self-kindness. Just as seeds need time to sprout and mature, the seeds of self-compassion also need time to establish themselves and thrive in your daily routines.

As we conclude this chapter, take a moment to consider how incorporating these self-compassion practices can be gentle yet potent tools in reshaping your self-relationship. Each small practice represents a step towards increased self-acceptance and a more fulfilling, peaceful life. Embrace these practices as guides towards deeper self-understanding and kindness, laying the groundwork for significant personal growth in the chapters ahead.

# CHAPTER 5

# STEPS TO SELF-ACCEPTANCE

*"Because true belonging only happens when we present our authentic,
imperfect selves to the world, our sense of belonging can never
be greater than our level of self-acceptance"*
– Brené Brown

Have you ever stood before a mirror, tracing the lines of your life's journey reflected there, and paused to ponder the meaning behind each line? Each one tells a story of laughter, worry, triumph, or challenge. Embracing these stories is at the heart of self-acceptance. It's about standing before that mirror and not merely seeing your reflection, but truly understanding and embracing the person looking back at you.

## 5.1 What Does it Mean to Accept Yourself?

Self-acceptance is deeply acknowledging and embracing all aspects of yourself—your strengths, weaknesses, successes, and failures. It's a complete acceptance that doesn't depend on achievements or external approval but is grounded in an intrinsic sense of your own value. Picture self-acceptance like returning to a house where you've always lived but never fully explored. It's about opening every door, looking into every corner, and choosing to cherish the home despite any imperfections it may have.

Take a moment to look back at the earlier chapters where you detailed the events of your past. Each of those moments, whether positive or challenging, has played a role in shaping who you are today. Embracing your past, with its ups and downs, isn't about giving in to fate but recognizing that these experiences form chapters in your life's story, not the entire narrative. Acceptance of your past doesn't mean you can't change; instead, it offers a stable base from which personal growth can flourish.

Radical acceptance is a powerful concept that encourages fully embracing everything about yourself—your emotions, mistakes, successes, and failures—without judgment, right now. Developed by psychologist Marsha Linehan as part of Dialectical Behavior Therapy, radical acceptance helps to reduce suffering from past events by fully accepting the reality of what has happened and ceasing to struggle against it. For example, if a past relationship left you heartbroken, radical acceptance involves acknowledging the pain and understanding how that experience has influenced your growth, without allowing it to control your future happiness.

Embarking on the journey of radical acceptance means examining your past and understanding how it has shaped the person you are today, without criticizing yourself but with compassion. It's about realizing that while you can't alter what has happened, you do have the ability to influence what comes next. The path to self-acceptance is demanding; it asks you to face aspects of yourself that you may have been avoiding. It's not about settling for who you are and stopping growth. Instead, it's recognizing that as you accept yourself as you are now, you also possess the potential to evolve in ways you desire.

Embracing self-acceptance means finding harmony with your reflections in the mirror. It involves breaking free from self-condemnation and embracing self-compassion instead. Here's an exercise to support your journey towards self-acceptance: Write a letter to yourself where you forgive yourself for everything—whether it's anger, mistakes, or past decisions. This simple act can be incredibly freeing, enabling you to release burdens you've carried and move forward with a lighter heart.

As you delve into this chapter, keep in mind that every stride toward self-acceptance is a stride toward liberation. It involves unlocking the doors within you that fear or shame may have closed, and realizing that each room, no matter how dark it once appeared, has windows ready to be opened to invite light in. Embrace yourself, your story, and your journey with all its imperfections, and observe how this acceptance not only changes your self-perception but also influences your interactions with the world around you.

## 5.2 Body Positivity: Loving the Skin You're In

In today's culture, the media often promotes an idealized body type, leading many of us, particularly women, to grapple with body image concerns. Research shows that nearly 91% of women are dissatisfied with their bodies and turn to dieting in pursuit of an ideal physique. However, only a small 5% naturally possess the body shape typically depicted in American media. This disparity between reality and societal expectations can profoundly impact self-esteem and mental well-being.

Reflecting on your own experiences, consider the messages about body image and beauty you encountered while growing up. Perhaps a family member frequently emphasized the need to lose weight, or a parent placed great importance on physical appearance, subtly implying that one's worth and acceptance were linked to how they looked. Such influences can shape our perceptions of ourselves and others, influencing our self-esteem and relationship with our bodies.

These experiences highlight how deeply familial and societal expectations shape our body image. The constant emphasis on conforming to a specific appearance can sow seeds of dissatisfaction and self-criticism, making it difficult to appreciate our bodies as they are. Understanding the origins of these perceptions is crucial for starting to challenge and change them. It helps us recognize that these views aren't inherently ours but are ideas we've been conditioned to adopt. This awareness is the first step in dismantling negative body image and fostering a healthier relationship with ourselves.

Challenging societal beauty standards is essential in fostering body positivity. Every day, we're inundated with images and messages that promote a narrow definition of beauty—a definition that is not only unrealistic but often unhealthy. Begin by critically examining these norms. When you encounter an advertisement or a fashion magazine, ask yourself, "Who benefits from me believing I need to conform to this standard?" This critical reflection can help you begin to separate your self-worth from these imposed ideals. By questioning and challenging these standards, you empower yourself to embrace a more authentic and inclusive view of beauty.

To cultivate a healthier body image, start incorporating body acceptance exercises into your daily routine. One effective practice is the mirror exercise. Stand before a mirror, look into your eyes, and give yourself compliments. Direct your attention to different parts of your body, appreciating each for what it enables you to do. Thank your legs for supporting you, your arms for embracing loved ones, your eyes for allowing you to see the world. This exercise shifts your focus away from how your body appears to what it accomplishes, promoting appreciation rather than criticism.

Another powerful practice is to keep a body gratitude journal. Each day, write down three things you appreciate about your body. Focus on its functionality, strength, or aspects of its appearance that bring you joy. As you continue this practice, your journal will become a meaningful reminder of your body's worth and resilience. It can help counteract negative thoughts that often occupy your mind, fostering a more positive and appreciative relationship with your body over time.

Lastly, celebrate the diversity of human beauty by exposing yourself to a wide range of body types, especially those that are often overlooked in mainstream media. Follow body-positive influencers, explore literature that embraces diverse physical forms, and engage in communities that promote body acceptance. By immersing yourself in these diverse representations, you can reinforce the understanding that beauty is not confined to a single, narrow standard but exists across a spectrum where each individual shines uniquely. This broader perspective encourages appreciation for all body types and supports a more inclusive view of beauty.

As a health and wellness coach, I do want to make an important note here. Just because we are working to accept and love ourselves and our bodies exactly as they are, that doesn't mean that we don't have to take care of them and try to be as healthy as we can. In an ideal world, we want both. Accept our bodies for what they are and all they do for us and then do our part to make sure we take care of them and keep them as healthy as we can.

You are going to notice a trend here again because addressing common body image issues includes actively managing negative thoughts. When you notice yourself falling into self-criticism, try applying the STOP technique:

**S - Stop:** Pause whatever you're doing.

**T - Take a breath:** Take a deep breath to center yourself.

**O - Observe your thoughts:** Notice the negative thoughts without judgment.

**P - Proceed with something positive:** Replace those thoughts with affirmations or a body gratitude practice.

This method helps interrupt the cycle of negative thinking and empowers you to cultivate a more positive mindset about your body.

By embracing these practices, you embark on a transformative journey where body positivity becomes more than just an idea—it becomes a lived experience. This shift enhances not only your self-esteem but also aligns you with a path where self-love and acceptance are central to how you perceive and treat yourself. As you delve deeper into these practices, let them foster a friendship with your body—one rooted in respect, appreciation, and deep care. Remember that the key to success is **consistently** changing your thoughts over and over until positive thoughts become your normal thoughts.

## 5.3 Celebrating Your Uniqueness: Beyond Comparisons

Have you ever found yourself scanning a room, comparing your outfit, your body, and everything else to those around you? Perhaps you've felt a pang of inadequacy when a friend shared a success story, wondering why your own achievements seem less impressive in comparison. This is a common experience in a world that often feels like a stage where everyone is watching and judging.

But here's the truth: comparison can rob you of joy and obscure the beautiful reality of who you truly are. Understanding and addressing the triggers of comparison is your initial step toward celebrating your unique self, free from the shadows cast by comparison.

Let's delve into the sources that often fuel the urge to compare ourselves with others. Social media, for instance, is a mixed blessing. It connects us with friends and family, yet it also presents a constant flow of carefully selected highlights from others' lives, which can trigger feelings of envy and inadequacy.

Additionally, peer groups and family expectations often unintentionally set up comparisons based on achievements and lifestyles. Recognizing these triggers is crucial because it enables you to step back and evaluate whether your comparisons are motivating you positively or simply fostering self-doubt.

For example, if you find yourself scrolling through social media and feeling worse with each post, it may be time to reconsider how you interact with these platforms. Setting boundaries on your social media usage or curating your feed to include more positive and uplifting content can shield you from the onslaught of comparison triggers. This proactive approach helps prioritize your mental well-being and encourages a healthier perspective on self-worth.

Embracing and celebrating your individuality is the antidote to the negativity of comparison. Begin by creating a list—not of your perceived shortcomings or what you lack, but of every trait, talent, and quirk that defines who you are. Include things like your ability to make people laugh, your talent for solving puzzles quickly, your passion for painting, or even your unique laugh. These are not just characteristics; they are the chapters of your life story that make you uniquely yourself. Celebrating these differences involves shifting your focus from what you might think you lack to the abundance of qualities you uniquely possess. It's about transforming the narrative from comparison to appreciation of your own individuality.

Expressing your individuality is a potent means to reconnect with your true self. This might manifest through fashion choices that reflect your personal style rather than following trends. It could also emerge in hobbies that deeply resonate with your soul, rather than pursuing activities merely because they are popular.

When you allow your authentic self to shine, you not only feel more genuine but also attract people and opportunities that align with your true interests and values. This authenticity is liberating  it declares that you are not here to fade into the background but to paint your own vibrant and unique picture.

Embracing vulnerability is pivotal in this journey. When you shed the mask and reveal your true self, you invite others to understand and appreciate you for who you truly are, not for who you think you should be. This can be intimidating—vulnerability always is. However, the connections and experiences that arise from this openness are inevitably deeper and more rewarding. They are grounded in authenticity and fortified by the courage it takes to authentically embrace yourself.

As you navigate your day, practice these steps consciously. Recognize when comparison begins to infiltrate your thoughts, and gently redirect your focus to your own unique attributes and accomplishments. Remind yourself that your worth remains steadfast even when others excel. Remember, there's enough room for everyone to shine, and your light doesn't dim because others are glowing too. Continue nurturing your individual traits, letting them be the reasons you celebrate your journey every day. Embrace your uniqueness and let it illuminate your path forward.

## 5.4 Accepting Your Emotions: Techniques for Emotional Regulation

Understanding and managing your emotions is integral to self-acceptance. Emotional intelligence, a concept developed by psychologists John Mayer and Peter Salovey, refers to the ability to recognize, understand, and manage our own emotions, as well as to recognize, understand, and influence the emotions of others. Put simply, it's about being aware of your emotions and handling them in a constructive and mindful manner.

This awareness is crucial because emotions can cloud our judgment and lead to reactive behaviors that may not align with our true intentions or values.

Emotional intelligence forms the bedrock of self-acceptance as it enables you to comprehend and embrace your emotional intricacies rather than fearing or repressing them. For instance, acknowledging that feeling anxious about a new job is a normal response can empower you to manage that anxiety rather than letting it dominate you. By accepting and addressing your emotions, you validate your experiences and affirm your emotional landscape as a vital aspect of your identity. This approach fosters a deeper understanding of yourself and cultivates a more authentic sense of self-acceptance.

Now, let's look at some practical tools for managing your emotions, especially when they feel overwhelming. Deep breathing exercises are a straightforward yet effective technique to begin with. When you're caught up in strong emotions such as anger or anxiety, take a moment to concentrate on your breathing. Inhale deeply through your nose, allowing your stomach to rise, and exhale slowly through your mouth. Repeat this a few times. This exercise can lessen the intensity of your emotions, providing you with a clearer mindset to respond calmly.

Mindfulness and meditation are important for managing emotions as well. Mindfulness means being fully present in the moment, without judging what's happening. When emotions come up, instead of reacting right away or feeling overwhelmed, mindfulness teaches you to observe these feelings. It's like stepping back and watching your emotions pass by, similar to clouds moving across the sky—they're there, but they don't take over your entire view.

Meditation, especially mindfulness meditation, helps strengthen mindfulness. It encourages awareness and focused attention. You can start with just five minutes a day, sitting quietly and focusing on your breath or repeating a calming word. Whenever your mind wanders, gently bring it back to your breath or mantra.

Promoting emotional acceptance is crucial. Society often looks down on expressing negative emotions such as sadness or fear, but suppressing these feelings can cause more emotional distress. Instead, it's important to acknowledge and express your emotions in healthy ways. If you feel sad, give yourself permission to cry or discuss your feelings with a trusted friend. When frustrated, consider writing down your thoughts or engaging in physical activity to release built-up tension. Allowing yourself to feel and express these emotions validates their significance and affirms your right to experience them, which is essential for self-acceptance and emotional regulation.

The ultimate goal is building emotional resilience which means improving how you handle challenges and recover from setbacks. It's about seeing challenges as chances to grow and keeping a positive outlook. This doesn't mean ignoring difficulties but understanding them in a broader context where growth and learning are achievable. For example, if a work project doesn't go as expected, rather than being hard on yourself, reflect on what you can gain from the experience and how it can enhance your skills in your job.

Incorporating these practices into your daily routine not only improves your ability to handle and express emotions in a healthy way but also strengthens your self-awareness and self-acceptance. Emotions are a natural part of being human—they connect us, motivate us, and offer valuable lessons. By embracing your emotions with wisdom and kindness, you pave the way for a more genuine and satisfying journey of self-acceptance. Remember, each emotion you experience contributes to the melody of your life; it's within your power to harmonize these emotions by understanding and guiding them intentionally.

## 5.5 The Power of Saying 'No': Practicing Assertiveness

Imagine standing firm with confidence, expressing your needs and desires without hesitation or fear of upsetting others. This is assertiveness—an important skill that means communicating your thoughts and feelings directly, honestly, and respectfully. It fosters self-respect and self-acceptance by empowering you to make decisions based on your values and needs, rather than conforming to expectations that don't benefit you.

Assertiveness and aggression are often confused, yet they differ fundamentally. Assertiveness involves confidently and respectfully expressing your true self. It focuses on negotiating and seeking solutions that consider both your needs and the rights of others, fostering balanced and healthy relationships. In contrast, aggression involves imposing your will on others without regard for their feelings or rights. For instance, if a friend frequently cancels plans at the last minute, an assertive approach might be, "I feel disappointed when our plans are canceled. Can we find a solution that works well for both of us?" This response acknowledges your feelings while also respecting your friend's circumstances.

To help you develop this skill, let's practice with practical scenarios and responses. Imagine a common work situation: your boss asks you to take on another project when your workload is already full. An assertive response could be, "I recognize the significance of this project, but I'm currently at capacity with [specific tasks]. Could we discuss priorities or possibly delegate some tasks to ensure everything is completed effectively?" This approach clearly communicates your boundaries while showing your willingness to find a solution that benefits everyone involved.

Maybe you're facing a persistent relative who wants you to attend an event you're not interested in. A polite yet firm response could be, 'Thank you for inviting me, but I can't make it this time. Let's catch up soon!' This shows appreciation for their invitation while respectfully declining.

Practicing these scenarios can greatly increase your confidence in dealing with similar situations in your everyday life. It reinforces your grasp of assertiveness and helps you internalize assertive responses. You can role-play with a friend or practice in front of a mirror, adjusting your tone and body language to show confidence without being aggressive.

Being assertive offers benefits that go beyond immediate interactions. It boosts your self-confidence by affirming your ability to advocate for your beliefs and needs. This improvement in self-assurance enhances relationships through clear, honest communication that fosters trust and prevents misunderstandings. Additionally, others come to respect your opinions and decisions more, appreciating your open and respectful communication style.

Embracing assertiveness marks a transformative leap toward recognizing your self-worth and living in alignment with your desires and values. It's about granting yourself the freedom to be authentic, unapologetically. As you consistently apply assertiveness in your daily interactions, you'll discover that it not only enriches your relationships but also advances your path towards self-acceptance and empowerment. By confidently saying 'no' when needed, you affirmatively say 'yes' to a more genuine and fulfilling life.

# CHAPTER 6

# BUILDING SELF-CONFIDENCE

*"No one can make you feel inferior without your consent"*
— Eleanor Roosevelt

Have you ever thought about how confidence grows? It's a lot like tending a garden: you need to prepare, care, and create the right environment for it to thrive. Building confidence isn't just about feeling good—it's about laying a solid foundation that helps you grow and handle life's challenges confidently. Let's explore some practical steps you can take to develop this important quality. By nurturing your self-perception, you can turn it into fertile ground for self-assurance and personal success.

## 6.1 Setting Achievable Goals for Confidence Building

### The SMART criteria

Boosting self confidence often starts with setting clear, achievable goals. You might wonder how setting goals relates to confidence. It's really about daring to explore new paths and committing to personal growth. By setting goals, embracing challenges, and celebrating successes, you uncover your potential and build self-esteem. One effective tool for goal-setting is the SMART criteria. Each letter in SMART—specific, measurable, achievable, relevant, and time-bound—helps ensure your goals are well-defined and within reach.

## *Let's break this down:*

- **Specific:** Define your goals clearly to avoid confusion. Instead of a general aim like "increasing confidence," specify what confidence means to you. For example, it could involve participating more actively in meetings or forging new connections at social events.

- **Measurable:** Establish benchmarks to track your progress. For instance, if you aim to be more engaged in meetings, set a measurable goal such as contributing at least two ideas in each session.

- **Achievable:** Ensure your goals are realistic, taking into account your resources and limitations. If the idea of public speaking feels overwhelming, aiming to lead a large conference might be too ambitious at first. Begin with smaller, more attainable steps.

- **Relevant**: Ensure your objectives align with your broader life goals. Consider how improving your public speaking skills contributes to your career or personal development.

- **Time-bound:** Setting a deadline gives you motivation and a clear timeline for achieving your goals. Establish a target date, whether it's within a week, a month, or a year. Focus on smaller, short-term goals that lead to accomplishing larger, long-term objectives.

Often, when setting goals, we focus on the desired outcome without considering the specifics needed to achieve it. Setting goals without a plan is like navigating without a compass. To help you effectively set goals for building confidence, let's create a SMART goal together.

Suppose your goal is to enhance your public speaking abilities. A vague objective might be, "I want to get better at public speaking." Applying the SMART framework, we refine it as follows:

1. **Specific:** Actively participate in team meetings and join a local public speaking club.

2. **Measurable**: Aim to contribute at least once in every weekly team meeting and attend a public speaking club twice a month.

3. **Achievable:** Given your current commitments, these goals are realistic and allow time for preparation and finding a suitable club.

4. **Relevant:** Improving public speaking skills will enhance your communication abilities, benefiting both professional and personal development.

5. **Time-bound:** Set a goal to achieve this within the next three months, with weekly progress assessments.

As a final goal, instead of simply wanting to get better at public speaking, your goal could be: "I aim to enhance my public speaking skills by actively participating in every team meeting and joining a local speaking club twice a month." This approach provides specific actions to motivate and guide your progress.

Setting goals can sometimes feel intimidating because we fear not achieving them and feeling like we've failed. To overcome this, I prefer to view goal-setting as an experiment. Once you've set a goal and tried sticking to it for a set period, the next step is to assess what happened. It's not about success or failure; it's about understanding the experience and figuring out how to improve your chances of success. If you achieved your goal, think about what contributed to your success. Can these factors be applied to other goals? If you didn't achieve your goal, analyze what went wrong. Were there specific challenges or triggers that made it difficult? Could you make adjustments, set reminders, or find ways to make the goal more enjoyable? Approaching goals this way shifts the focus from failure to learning and self-compassion.

Building confidence requires patience, dedication, and a willingness to explore new territories. Begin this journey with small steps that gently push you out of your comfort zone. For instance, if you aim to build new connections, start by having short, meaningful conversations with colleagues or people you meet daily. As you become more comfortable, gradually expand to larger social events. This gradual progression helps you build confidence step by step, enhancing your sense of self-assurance along the way.

As you progress, reflecting on your achievements becomes crucial. After each interaction or accomplishment, take a moment to identify what helped you succeed. Was it preparation, support from a friend, or something else that made you feel more at ease? Recognizing these factors not only enhances your confidence but also prepares you to replicate your successes. When working to boost your self-confidence, think of each goal as a seed. By setting specific, measurable, achievable, relevant, and time-bound objectives, and by gradually challenging yourself and reflecting on your progress, these seeds can grow into a thriving garden of confidence and self-assurance.

## 6.2 The Role of Body Language in Self-Assurance

Do you ever walk into a room full of people and suddenly feel the urge to blend into the background? Or in conversations, do you find yourself avoiding eye contact or slouching? These actions aren't random—they reflect our inner feelings and significantly influence both our self-perception and how others perceive us. Body language holds immense power; it communicates more than words and profoundly affects our sense of confidence.

Research in nonverbal communication highlights how our posture can dramatically impact both our self-confidence and how others perceive us. Social psychologist Amy Cuddy has famously discussed the concept of "power poses," which can enhance confidence by affecting hormone levels. These poses can increase testosterone, linked to assertiveness, while decreasing cortisol, associated with stress. By adopting postures that convey confidence, you not only appear more assured but can also genuinely feel more confident.

Let's explore these power poses. One well-known pose is the "Victory" pose—standing tall with hands raised above your head as if celebrating a win. This pose evokes feelings of success and triumph, which can psychologically impact your confidence just by holding it. Another effective pose is the "Wonder Woman" stance—feet apart, hands on hips. This posture signifies strength and readiness to tackle challenges head-on. Try practicing these poses in private for a few minutes before situations where you need a confidence boost. You might be pleasantly surprised by how much more empowered and assured you feel afterward.

Incorporating confident body language into everyday situations can significantly influence both your interactions and your self-confidence. For example, maintaining eye contact during conversations signals engagement and assertiveness. This not only projects confidence to others but also reinforces your own perception of competence. Likewise, using assertive hand gestures while speaking can lend more authority to your words, enhancing your presence in every interaction. These subtle yet powerful cues can shape how you're perceived and how you feel about yourself in various contexts.

To apply this in real situations, let's try a few role-play exercises. Picture yourself at a networking event. Instead of folding your arms or checking your phone, stand with an open posture—shoulders back, head held high, and hands either at your sides or using gestures as you speak. During conversations, maintain consistent eye contact, nod to indicate you're listening attentively, and offer a genuine smile. These subtle yet deliberate gestures can noticeably enhance how approachable and confident you come across to others.

Let's consider another scenario, such as a job interview. When you enter the room, walk in with a firm and confident stride. Offer a strong handshake, which universally signals confidence and readiness. During the interview, sit upright in your chair, lean slightly forward to demonstrate interest, and use appropriate hand gestures to emphasize your responses. These actions not only convey confidence but also showcase your enthusiasm for the position you're seeking.

Remember, the concept of "fake it till you make it" is pivotal in understanding body language. Even if you don't initially feel completely confident, behaving as if you are can gradually lead to genuine self-assurance. Body language and emotions have a reciprocal relationship—they influence each other. By intentionally practicing confident body language, you're not only preparing to appear assured but also creating a pathway to genuinely embody confidence over time. It's about using your body's cues to reinforce positive feelings and behaviors, ultimately shaping your mindset and interactions positively.

So, next time you need a confidence boost, remember your body language tools. Stand tall, hold your head high, and let your body show confidence. As you practice, these actions will become natural, changing not just how others see you, but also how you see yourself.

## 6.3 Affirmations for Daily Confidence

Imagine starting each day with a gentle reminder of your worth and capabilities, and the bright possibilities ahead. This is the essence of affirmations—simple yet powerful statements that can change your mindset, strengthen your self-belief, and push away doubt. Affirmations aren't just hopeful words; they are daily tools for empowerment, designed to ground you in positivity and boost your confidence.

Affirmations influence your subconscious mind, gradually reshaping your thoughts. Think of them as seeds of positivity planted in your mind's garden. With regular care, these seeds grow, transforming your inner landscape from self-doubt to confidence. Effective affirmations should be personal, framed in the present tense, and full of emotion. For example, instead of saying, "I will be confident," say, "I am confident in my abilities and choices." This present-tense phrasing declares your current reality, making it more powerful.

Integrating affirmations into your daily routine can be simple and transformative. One effective method is to include them in your morning routine. As you get ready for the day, stand in front of a mirror, look yourself in the eye, and recite your affirmations. This act of speaking to your reflection reinforces the message, making it more impactful. Alternatively, you can incorporate affirmations into your meditation sessions. As you sit in silence and focus on your breath, silently repeat your affirmations once you feel centered. This can deepen the sense of peace and confidence you carry throughout the day.

Another practical approach is to place visual reminders of your affirmations where you'll see them often, such as on your bathroom mirror, car dashboard, or phone background. Each time you see these reminders, pause, recite the affirmation, and take a deep breath. This practice keeps your focus on positive self-talk throughout the day, gradually shifting your mindset towards greater self-assurance.

The power of affirmations isn't just anecdotal; it's reflected in many personal stories. Take Anna, a young graphic designer who struggled with severe self-doubt about her artistic talents. Despite receiving positive feedback, she couldn't shake the feeling that she wasn't good enough. When she started using affirmations daily, things began to change. Every morning, she would say, "I am a talented and creative designer. My work brings joy and beauty to the world." Over time, these words reshaped how she viewed herself and her work. Her confidence grew, and she began to take on more challenging projects, further reinforcing her belief in her capabilities

Affirmations are more than just words; they are commitments to yourself. They are daily reminders of your strengths and the incredible potential you possess. As you continue to use affirmations, remember that each repetition is a step towards a more confident and empowered you. Let these simple statements be your daily companions, gently guiding you toward a life where self-doubt is replaced by unwavering self-belief and confidence in your abilities.

## 6.4 Overcoming Social Anxiety Through Self-Talk

Social anxiety is that lingering fear that whispers you're not quite right for the room, that your words might stumble or your voice might shake, and everyone will notice. It's a common experience, affecting many of us in varying degrees, from butterflies in the stomach before a social event to more debilitating effects that can hinder everyday interactions. Recognizing social anxiety involves tuning into the symptoms—perhaps you feel a rapid heartbeat, excessive sweating, or a mind that races with worry about upcoming social interactions. To gauge its impact, consider how often these feelings occur and whether they prevent you from participating in activities you would otherwise enjoy.

Now, let's talk about reshaping those anxious thoughts through a powerful tool called cognitive restructuring. This method involves identifying and challenging the irrational beliefs that fuel your anxiety. It requires persistence because these patterns are often ingrained. For instance, if you believe, "I always say the wrong thing," challenge this by recalling times when you communicated well. Replace that negative thought with something more balanced like, "Sometimes I'm not as articulate as I'd like, but many times I express myself just fine."

To bolster your confidence during social interactions, try crafting specific phrases or mantras that reaffirm your abilities. Before stepping into a social setting, you might repeat to yourself, "I am interesting, and people enjoy my company." These affirmations help prepare your mind to enter interactions with a positive, self-assured mindset.

Gradual exposure is crucial for managing social anxiety. This involves systematically facing the social situations that scare you, rather than avoiding them. Start with less intimidating interactions, like saying hello to a neighbor, and gradually progress to more challenging scenarios, such as initiating a conversation at a large gathering. Each small victory adds up, boosting your confidence and diminishing the grip of anxiety over time.

Through these techniques, you can transform the way you see yourself and social interactions. Instead of viewing social settings as battlegrounds, they can become playgrounds where you explore connections and express your true self with less fear and more joy. This shift in perspective fosters a more positive and fulfilling experience in social situations.

As a final reminder, recognize that the journey to increased self-confidence is unique to you and unfolds gradually. Each step you take builds upon the last, contributing to a stronger, more confident version of yourself. Moving forward, we will explore and address several personal barriers that may hinder self-love, ensuring that your path to self-empowerment is holistic and thorough.

# MAKE A DIFFERENCE WITH YOUR REVIEW
## UNLOCK THE POWER OF GENEROSITY

*"True generosity is an offering; given freely and*
*out of pure love. No strings attached."*
– Suze Orman

Generosity not only enriches our lives but also extends them. If there's a chance to tap into that magic today, why not seize it?

Here's a small favor I'm hoping you'll consider…

Would you help someone just like you were—eager to grow and transform, but unsure where to begin?

Our goal with Self-Love for Women is clear: to reach and uplift as many women as possible. But we can only spread this message with your support. That's right, your help can extend the reach of this empowering guide to countless others.

Most people choose books based on their reviews, so here's where you come in. I'm asking you, on behalf of someone out there who needs this book but hasn't found it yet:

Could you spare a moment to leave a review?

This simple act requires no money, just a minute of your time, yet it can profoundly impact another woman's journey toward self-love and confidence. Your review can:

- Empower another woman to start her journey of self-acceptance.
- Support continuous personal growth and healing.
- Encourage someone to take the first step toward lasting self-worth.
- Inspire more stories of transformation and triumph.

To leave your review, just scan the QR code below:

If you believe in lifting others as you climb, then you're exactly who I hoped would pick up this book. Welcome to the community of changemakers.

I'm grateful for your support and excited to accompany you through the next steps of your personal journey.

Thank you from the bottom of my heart. Let's continue making a positive impact together.

Your ally in self-love,

*Whitney Prude*

# CHAPTER 7

# UNDERSTANDING PERSONAL BARRIERS

*"You are braver than you believe, stronger than you seem,*
*and smarter than you think."*
– Joseph B. Wirthlin

Have you ever felt like you don't quite fit into your own life, watching others succeed and wondering if they have some secret you're missing? It's a troubling feeling that sneaks in when you acknowledge your achievements but still feel unsure of yourself, or when you dismiss your successes as mere luck or good timing. This is impostor syndrome—a psychological experience where you question your abilities and worry about being exposed as a "fraud." It's akin to standing on a stage where you feel out of place, and every round of applause feels unwarranted. If this sounds familiar, know that you're not alone. This chapter explores not only imposter syndrome but many other challenging barriers that many women face on a regular basis.

## 7.1 Recognizing and Overcoming Impostor Syndrome

Impostor syndrome goes beyond mere insecurity; it's a profound sense of personal inadequacy that persists despite clear accomplishments. It shows up as persistent self-doubt and a feeling of intellectual dishonesty that overshadows any evidence of success or competence. For example, imagine you've been promoted at work. Instead of feeling excited, you might feel anxious, thinking, "I don't deserve this. What if they discover I'm not as capable as they think?" This syndrome deceives talented, accomplished individuals into believing they're unworthy and that their successes are merely accidental.

Feelings of inadequacy can be triggered in various ways, and identifying these triggers can provide valuable insights. Often, these feelings arise with new accomplishments or advancements—like starting a new job, receiving a promotion, or achieving success in academic or professional settings. It can feel like standing on the edge of a new horizon, questioning whether you've somehow tricked your way there. For many women, especially in male-dominated fields, these triggers are intensified by external skepticism about their abilities, which can lead to internalized self-doubt. Recognizing these triggers is the initial step toward overcoming them.

Addressing impostor syndrome involves a blend of self-reflection, practical tactics, and sometimes seeking support. One effective approach is to reframe your thinking to fully acknowledge and accept your accomplishments. Rather than attributing success to luck, affirm your readiness and capability, recognizing your hard work and dedication. Another powerful strategy is keeping a success journal. Record your achievements, the skills applied, and the value you contributed. Reviewing this journal reinforces your track record and bolsters confidence when self-doubt arises.

Drawing on the support of mentors is crucial in overcoming impostor syndrome. Mentors provide an external perspective on your abilities and journey, often highlighting your growth and achievements in ways you might overlook. They act as a mirror to your professional and personal development, especially when self-doubt clouds your own perception. However, the challenge lies in genuinely accepting and internalizing their feedback. It's common to deflect compliments, downplay achievements, or steer conversations away from your successes. To truly combat impostor syndrome, it's essential to resist these tendencies. Embrace positive feedback with a simple "thank you," allowing yourself to appreciate recognition without diminishing it. This practice isn't just about manners; it's a deliberate effort to retrain your mindset to acknowledge and celebrate your victories. As you learn to accept praise gracefully, you also confront and manage the inner doubts that undermine these moments. It's a continual process to quiet those self-critical voices, but over time, with persistence, they diminish, creating space for a narrative of empowerment and self-assurance to thrive.

If you've ever looked at my social media profiles, you might think, "She's achieved so much—she's smart, runs a successful business, and seems to have it all together." But assuming I'm completely free from impostor syndrome and overflowing with confidence would be far from accurate. My journey into entrepreneurship didn't start from ambition but from necessity. After earning a doctorate in pharmacy through years of hard work, I faced a severe illness that limited my ability to practice. With $200,000 in student loans looming and disability constraints, I was pushed to explore other paths. Starting my business was as simple as a $150 online transaction, instantly labeling me a business owner. This ease made me question, "Is it really this easy? Do I truly belong here?" These feelings of inadequacy have been constant companions since then. Despite significant growth in my business, confidence and a sense of having 'figured it all out' remain elusive. Every day brings new challenges and lessons in managing a growing enterprise. Yet, I've learned to embrace my achievements and the hard work behind them. While I don't have all the answers or run a flawless business, I no longer dwell on these imperfections. Instead, I celebrate my victories and focus on evolving into the business leader I aspire to be, one step at a time.

Let's draw more inspiration from Maya, a tech entrepreneur who grappled with impostor syndrome despite her startup's success. She candidly shared, "Whenever I was invited to speak at conferences, I felt like I didn't belong. I kept thinking they must have invited me by mistake." Recognizing the impact of impostor syndrome on her confidence, Maya began therapy to confront these feelings head-on. She adopted a practice of documenting every compliment and positive feedback she received at work. Over time, Maya found that these notes became tangible proof of her competence. Gradually, the self-doubting voice in her head started losing its power. Her journey highlights the transformative effect of acknowledging and internalizing positive feedback, paving the way for greater self-assurance and professional growth.

Another perspective comes from Ava, a novelist who struggled with feeling like she wasn't a "real" writer despite having published multiple books. Ava found solace and validation when she joined a writing group. Sharing her experiences with fellow writers made her realize that many others felt the same way, which helped her overcome the isolation of her feelings. Reflecting on this, Ava said, "Realizing that I wasn't alone in experiencing these doubts was incredibly liberating." Her story underscores the power of community and shared experiences in overcoming impostor syndrome and embracing one's identity as a writer.

In recounting these stories, we witness not only the challenges but also the paths toward overcoming the deeply ingrained beliefs that feed impostor syndrome. These stories serve as beacons of hope and practical guides for managing the self-doubt that often accompanies this syndrome. As you reflect on these insights, allow yourself to entertain the idea that you are precisely where you belong—not due to luck, but because of your hard work and competence. Embrace this chapter as a stride toward recognizing yourself as the capable and accomplished individual you truly are, free from the shadows of doubt that impostor syndrome can cast.

## 7.2 The Impact of Social Media on Self-Image

In an age where our daily lives are intertwined with digital interactions, it's crucial to consider that the average American spends about 2 hours and 3 minutes on social media each day. This substantial portion of our daily routine, dedicated to platforms meant to connect and entertain, also profoundly influences our self-perception and mental well-being. The constant stream of curated lives and perfect images can distort our sense of reality, creating standards that are not only unrealistic but often impossible to achieve.

Social media platforms offer numerous benefits, providing spaces for expression and connection. However, they also present a double-edged sword: fostering an environment where unrealistic portrayals of life are commonplace. These portrayals can lead us to question our achievements and physical appearance, subtly impacting our self-esteem and mental well-being. The "comparison trap," as it's known, is a genuine phenomenon where we measure our everyday lives against the edited highlights of others. This constant comparison can undermine our self-love and contentment with our own lives. Each like, comment, and share can become a yardstick by which we measure our worth, often forgetting that online content is often a selective portrayal of reality.

To navigate the digital landscape more mindfully, consider implementing these tips for healthier social media use. Start by setting clear boundaries. This could involve limiting your daily or weekly screen time or scheduling specific times each day to check social media. By controlling when and how you engage with these platforms, you reduce the risk of mindless scrolling and potential negative impacts on your mental health. Additionally, curate your social media feed intentionally. Follow accounts that inspire and uplift you, such as artists, thought leaders, or content creators who share enriching content. This selective approach transforms your feed into a source of motivation and positive energy, rather than one that drains you.

At age 21, my daily life revolved around Facebook. I found myself endlessly scrolling through friends' profiles, comparing my life to theirs, and seeking validation through likes and comments. This constant quest for social media affirmation began to stir anxiety within me as I realized I was capturing moments primarily for online approval rather than personal enjoyment. A turning point came when I acknowledged the toll this behavior was taking on my mental health. I made a conscious decision to step back from social media, choosing to live for myself rather than for the validation of others. The aftermath of this decision was liberating. Over nine years without social media, my self-confidence grew, and I learned to appreciate my own journey more deeply. Eventually, I returned to social media for business purposes, armed with the understanding that a healthy relationship with these platforms starts from a healthy internal state. I realized that my self-worth is not tied to online metrics. When you find fulfillment from within, the external validation offered by social media loses its power over your happiness.

If you're not ready to give up social media entirely as I did, I encourage you to consider digital detoxes—periods when you completely disconnect from social media. This could be for a weekend getaway or during vacation times. Taking these breaks helps reset your mental state and creates space to engage more deeply with the physical world around you. It's an opportunity to reconnect with yourself and others without the filter of digital interactions. If you're feeling adventurous, try extending these detoxes. For example, challenge yourself to a week or even a month without social media. This longer break can offer profound insights into how your life changes without the constant digital buzz. Consider keeping a journal during this time to reflect on your mood, relationships, and self-image when you step away from the online world.

By embracing these mindful practices, you're not just protecting your mental well-being but also taking back control of your self-worth from social media metrics. It's important to remember that your value isn't determined by online interactions, and real life is beautifully imperfect—something no filter or edit can capture. As you incorporate these practices into your life, let them serve as reminders that your truest self exists beyond the digital realm. You are fully capable and deserving of genuine happiness and self-acceptance.

## 7.3 Navigating the Pressure to Conform

When you consider the societal norms and expectations embedded in everyday life, it becomes clear how they can create significant obstacles to self-love. These societal pressures often promote conformity, subtly nudging you to conform to molds that may not align with your true self. The conflict between societal expectations and personal values can be especially challenging when you face decisions that pit conformity against authenticity.

Societal norms cover a broad range, from career choices and beauty standards to behavioral expectations and life milestones. The pressure to conform can create a sense of constant measurement against a universal standard, irrespective of your personal goals or situation. For example, the expectation to pursue a conventional career path can feel restrictive if your passion lies in a more unconventional or artistic field. Similarly, cultural definitions of beauty and success may drive a relentless pursuit of external validation, overshadowing your inherent value.

Empowering yourself to resist these pressures isn't about defying norms just for the sake of it; it's about asserting your right to define your own values and live authentically. This empowerment begins with a clear understanding of what truly matters to you. Engaging in self-reflection can be key to clarifying these personal values. Here's an exercise to help you get started: List out values that deeply resonate with you, such as creativity, independence, compassion, or integrity. For each value, jot down why it holds significance for you and how you perceive it might be challenged by societal expectations. This exercise not only helps crystallize your core values but also strengthens your determination to honor and uphold them in your life.

Finding like-minded communities is crucial for reinforcing your chosen values. These communities offer a supportive environment where your choices and beliefs are not only understood but celebrated. Whether it's a local meetup of creative professionals, an online forum for entrepreneurs, or a support group for single parents, these communities serve as a reminder that you are not alone in your journey toward living authentically.

Practicing assertiveness is essential when navigating societal pressures. It means clearly communicating your beliefs and making choices that align with your values, even when they differ from the norm. For example, if you feel pressured by family to pursue a specific career path, assertively expressing your own career ambitions can promote mutual understanding and respect. Assertiveness isn't about confrontation; it's about confidently and respectfully standing your ground. It allows you to assert your individuality while maintaining healthy relationships with those around you.

My personal journey with cultural and societal expectations had a profound impact on my sense of self. Growing up in a deeply religious household, I was immersed in a community with strict standards and norms. At first, I wholeheartedly embraced these expectations, equating them with being a good person. However, as I matured and confronted personal challenges like my parent's divorce and my own health issues, I started to question everything I had unquestioningly accepted before.

This period of doubt was incredibly isolating for me. I felt like I was letting down not only myself but also my family and community. The fear of disappointing those I loved was overwhelming. However, it was during this tumultuous time that I began to realize I had been living a life dictated more by external expectations than by my own truth. The journey to redefine my self-worth was challenging and lonely, yet it was also profoundly liberating. By prioritizing my authentic self over societal pressures, I gradually discovered peace and a sense of purpose that resonated deeply with who I truly am.

Navigating the pressure to conform is an ongoing journey of prioritizing authenticity over seeking approval. It means embracing the discomfort that can arise from standing apart rather than blending in. As you progress, keep in mind that every step towards honoring your true self is a step towards a life marked by genuine happiness and fulfillment. In a world that often encourages conformity, choosing to stay true to yourself is a courageous expression of self-love.

## 7.4 Breaking Free from Perfectionism

Life as a perfectionist typically means waking up each day with an unyielding taskmaster in your mind, insisting that everything you do—whether it's your work projects or your morning routine—must be flawless. It's not merely about having high standards; it's about setting expectations so impossibly high that they frequently result in nothing but stress and disappointment. Perfectionism isn't just about pursuing excellence; it casts a shadow over every endeavor, whispering that your efforts are perpetually inadequate.

Perfectionism often stems from early life experiences where love and approval were contingent on performance and achievement. It might have been a parent who overlooked your 98% on a test, emphasizing the missing 2%, or a competitive school environment where only top performers received recognition. These experiences can instill a belief that our worth is tied to flawless performance, embedding deep roots that influence how we perceive ourselves and our work.

But here's the twist: the expectations that drive perfectionism are often self-imposed. They are not external mandates but rules we set for ourselves, which means they can be revised. Recognizing that you have control over these standards is the initial step towards reducing perfectionism's influence. The key solution lies in adjusting your expectations. This doesn't imply lowering the bar unrealistically, but rather setting it at attainable levels where success is possible without compromising your well-being and leaving room for being human.

The impact of perfectionism goes beyond mental strain; it can lead to significant health issues such as anxiety, depression, and burnout. Constantly striving to meet impossible standards keeps your body in a state of perpetual stress, engaging in an exhausting battle you've imposed upon yourself. This chronic stress can deplete your energy, stifle your creativity, and diminish the satisfaction you derive from your hard-earned achievements.

To combat perfectionism, begin by establishing realistic goals. Break down larger tasks into manageable steps and celebrate each completion. This approach not only makes tasks less overwhelming but also offers frequent affirmations of your competence. Embrace mistakes as opportunities for learning. Every error presents insights, whether it's identifying a solution or discovering a new approach. Rather than criticizing yourself for mistakes, shift your focus to asking, "What can I learn from this?" This mindset fosters growth and resilience, easing the grip of perfectionism over time.

Another potent remedy for perfectionism is deliberately allowing yourself to not do things perfectly and embracing the discomfort that may arise. This practice can be profoundly freeing. For instance, send an email without endlessly checking it, or leave a minor imperfection in a project. Each instance reinforces the notion that imperfection is not only acceptable but also a natural part of life. This mindset grows stronger with practice, gradually reducing the anxiety associated with the need to be flawless. Over time, you'll find yourself more at ease with imperfection, fostering greater creativity and peace of mind.

Breaking free from perfectionism is about setting realistic and empowering standards that allow you to excel while embracing the journey itself. It's not about lowering your expectations but rather freeing them from the constraints of unattainable perfection. Striving for excellence involves finding that balance where you can give your best effort without sacrificing your well-being or joy in the process. It's about celebrating progress and learning from each experience, whether it's a success or a learning opportunity. In our ongoing exploration, we'll delve deeper into understanding and dismantling personal barriers, discovering how these insights can pave the way for greater self-love and fulfillment. This journey is about growth, resilience, and finding authenticity in every step forward.

# CHAPTER 8

# CULTIVATING HEALTHY RELATIONSHIPS

*"The way we communicate with others and ourselves*
*ultimately determines the quality of our lives."*
– Tony Robbins

U nderstanding the true nature of your relationships is essential for self-love. Sometimes, the bonds we have with partners, family, and friends might not be as nurturing as we think. Our close connections can blind us to the harmful ways these people might treat us, making it easy to ignore or justify toxic behaviors. This chapter encourages you to look closely and assess if your relationships genuinely support your well-being and journey to self-love. Realizing that some connections might be unhealthy is hard but necessary for protecting your emotional health and creating space for more fulfilling interactions.

## 8.1 Identifying and Exiting Toxic Relationships

### Recognizing the Shadows: What Constitutes a Toxic Relationship?

Toxic relationships consistently leave you feeling drained, unworthy, and diminished. They are marked by behaviors that undermine your well-being. Key elements include manipulation, where your emotions are controlled to suit someone else's needs, constant criticism that erodes your self-esteem, and a lack of respect that diminishes your worth. Recognizing these patterns is the first step toward reclaiming your peace and well-being.

### Signs and Symptoms: How Do You Know You're in a Toxic Relationship?

The signs can be subtle or glaringly obvious. You might find yourself constantly anxious about interactions with a particular person, always on edge, trying to anticipate their moods or reactions. Your self-worth might feel like it's taken a hit, leaving you doubting your value more often than not. Feeling perpetually drained after spending time with someone is also a red flag. These relationships can leave you feeling isolated from others as if you're stuck in an emotional quagmire with no clear way out.

### The Narcissist in Disguise: Identifying Narcissistic Behaviors

Understanding narcissism is crucial in identifying toxic relationships, especially those that may not seem harmful at first. Narcissists often charm their way into your life with grand gestures and apparent self-confidence. Over time, their true nature emerges through self-serving and manipulative actions. Common signs include a lack of empathy, a deep need for admiration, and a habit of belittling others to elevate themselves. If these behaviors sound familiar in your relationships, it might be time to look deeper and consider that you could be dealing with a narcissist.

## *Crafting Your Exit: Strategies for Leaving Toxic Relationships*

Deciding to leave a toxic relationship is a brave and essential step for your mental and emotional well-being. Start by seeking support from trusted friends, family, or professionals who can offer guidance and emotional assistance. Next, set clear and firm boundaries. Identify the behaviors you will no longer accept and communicate these boundaries assertively. If the toxic relationship involves a family member, complete separation may not be possible, but you can still protect yourself by establishing strong boundaries and learning to say no. In cases of intense emotional manipulation, seeking professional help might be necessary to ensure a safe and healthy exit.

## *After the Storm: Focusing on Self-Care*

Once you've left a toxic relationship, the journey of healing begins. Self-care is crucial. Engage in activities that restore your energy and bring you joy, such as yoga, reading, or spending time in nature—whatever soothes your soul. Reflective practices like journaling can also be therapeutic, helping you process your emotions and regain your balance. Remember, every step you take after a toxic relationship is a step toward a healthier, more empowered you.

In navigating these waters, remember that recognizing and leaving toxic relationships is not only about removing negativity from your life but also about making room for healthier, more fulfilling connections. It's about prioritizing your well-being and affirming your worth. As you turn the page on these harmful relationships, you open up a new chapter where respect, love, and positivity can flourish.

## 8.2 Navigating Co-dependency and Finding Independence

Co-dependency is like walking through life feeling like you're not just holding your own hand, but also clutching tightly to someone else's—so tightly that you can't tell where you end and they begin. This image captures the essence of co-dependency, a relational dynamic where one person's needs and behaviors are excessively tied to another's. In a co-dependent relationship, your mood, happiness, and identity might heavily depend on the other person, making it challenging to recognize where they end and you begin.

Co-dependency often feels like love or simply being a good partner or family member. You might find yourself constantly making sacrifices for someone else's happiness or struggling to say no when something doesn't feel right because their needs always overshadow your own. It's like living in a cycle where your own voice gets quieter and quieter. These relationships can occur with anyone important in your life—partners, parents, siblings, or close friends. Signs of co-dependency include difficulty making decisions without the other person's input, valuing their approval more than your own, and feeling trapped in the relationship or worrying about being abandoned.

The roots of co-dependent behavior often stem from a lack of self-love. If deep down you don't feel you're enough by yourself, you might unconsciously seek out relationships where you make yourself indispensable by always being the caretaker, pleaser, or problem solver. In these roles, you might feel a temporary sense of worthiness from being needed, but this often comes at the cost of your own well-being and independence.

Enhancing self-love is crucial for breaking away from co-dependent behaviors. It starts with recognizing and affirming your own worth independently of your relationships. When you begin to cherish your own needs, desires, and well-being, you create a shift that reduces the tendency to revolve your life around someone else. This transformation doesn't mean you care less about others; it means you are starting to honor your own life as equally important.

The journey to overcoming co-dependency involves cultivating practices that reinforce your independence and self-sufficiency. Engaging in hobbies that connect you with your passions and interests can be a powerful way to strengthen your sense of self. Whether it's painting, hiking, reading, or any other activity you do just for yourself, these are not just hobbies—they're affirmations of your individuality.

Setting personal goals is another crucial strategy. These goals should focus on your personal growth, not just on how you can better serve others. Whether it's pursuing a new career path, learning a new skill, or improving your physical health, these goals help shape a life that feels fulfilling and meaningful on your own terms.

Seeking therapy or coaching can be incredibly beneficial, especially if the roots of your co-dependency are deep-seated. A therapist can help you unravel the patterns that have kept you in co-dependent cycles and provide you with tools to establish healthier relationships.

Celebrating independence in your relationships means understanding that true love and care involve supporting each other's growth without losing yourself in someone else's needs. When both partners can stand independently yet choose to stand together, the relationship becomes a partnership of mutual respect and support. It's about recognizing your own completeness and choosing to share your life with others from a place of strength and wholeness.

In healthier dynamics, each person brings their complete self to the relationship, without fear of being overshadowed or losing their identity. This shift not only strengthens the relationship but also enriches each person's life deeply. As you embrace independence and nurture self-love, your relationships naturally evolve to reflect this new foundation—one grounded in the joy of sharing rather than the fear of losing oneself.

## 8.3 Communicating Boundaries with Love

Imagine sitting down with a friend over coffee, enjoying the cozy ambiance and the pleasure of good company. As your conversation progresses, your friend asks you for a favor that makes you uneasy. This moment, though seemingly minor, is a crucial juncture—do you agree despite your discomfort, or do you voice your true feelings? This scenario illustrates the importance of setting boundaries, a skill that not only conserves your energy but also strengthens your relationships by fostering honesty and mutual respect.

Boundaries are the lines we set around ourselves to define our comfort levels and how we expect to be treated by others. They are vital for preserving self-respect and ensuring that our relationships are mutually supportive. Without clear boundaries, we may feel overwhelmed, taken advantage of, or lose sight of our own needs amidst those of others. Setting boundaries is not a one-time event but an ongoing process that adapts to our evolving needs and relationships. It involves understanding your limits and effectively communicating them, requiring clarity, assertiveness, and consistency.

To start setting boundaries, begin by identifying what is truly important to you—your values, needs, and priorities. Reflect on past interactions that left you feeling uncomfortable or drained. What were the common elements in these situations? Perhaps you consistently took on tasks at work that overloaded your schedule, or maybe you have a family member who frequently invaded your personal space. Recognizing these patterns is your initial step toward making a change.

Once you've identified your boundaries, the next step is to communicate them clearly and assertively. This involves expressing your needs directly and respectfully, without feeling the need to apologize. For instance, if a colleague routinely expects you to take on their responsibilities at work, you could say, "I understand you need assistance, but I need to prioritize my own projects right now. Let's explore ways to distribute tasks more evenly." This statement is clear and respectful, firmly setting a boundary while also acknowledging the other person's needs.

Practicing assertive communication is key to ensuring that your boundaries are not only heard but also respected. It involves using "I" statements that focus on your feelings rather than accusing or blaming the other person. For example, you might say, "I feel overwhelmed when I take on extra tasks without notice. I would appreciate more advanced communication so I can better manage my workload." This approach keeps the conversation constructive and focused on finding solutions that work for both parties.

Setting boundaries can indeed be difficult with close friends and family due to deep emotional connections. In these situations, it's important to be gentle yet firm. Explain why the boundary is important to you and reassure them that it's about meeting your needs, not rejecting them. For example, if you have a friend who frequently drops by unannounced, you could say, "I love spending time with you, but I really need some notice before visits so I can be fully present for our time together." This approach shows respect for both your needs and your relationship, fostering understanding and mutual respect.

Maintaining boundaries is just as crucial as setting them. This involves consistently upholding your boundaries when they are challenged and communicating any changes if your needs evolve. It also means respecting others' boundaries, creating a balanced relationship where both parties feel valued and respected.

In situations where boundaries are repeatedly disregarded, it may be necessary to reassess the relationship or seek external support such as counseling, particularly if the relationship affects your mental health. Remember, setting and maintaining boundaries is fundamental to self love and relationship well-being. It enables you to honor and nurture both yourself and your relationships, fostering mutual respect and care.

## | 8.4 The Importance of Supportive Networks

Supportive networks can feel like you're in a room filled with warmth and light, surrounded by people who genuinely celebrate your successes and provide comfort in times of struggle. Such environments consist of individuals who not only understand and respect each other but actively contribute to each other's growth through encouragement, advice, and tangible support. These relationships are grounded in mutual respect and positive reinforcement, fostering a dynamic where each person both gives and receives, enhancing the collective resilience and joy of the group.

Supportive networks are invaluable not only in times of celebration but also in moments of challenge. They act as a cushion against life's setbacks, offering comfort and resilience. When surrounded by supportive individuals, you're more likely to bounce back from difficulties more effectively. Shared joy is another beautiful aspect of these relationships; achievements are celebrated not with envy but with genuine happiness, amplifying your sense of fulfillment and belonging. This sense of community is crucial as it fosters a feeling of being part of something larger than oneself, which is deeply affirming and uplifting.

Building such a network begins with being intentional about the environments you engage with. Places where people gather with a focus on personal growth—such as workshops, classes, or local meet-ups—often cultivate supportive relationships. Online platforms can also serve as a starting point to connect with like-minded individuals, but the goal should be to transition these digital interactions into real-world connections whenever possible. Deepening existing relationships is equally important. This could involve spending more time with a colleague or friend you connect with and opening up about your experiences more authentically. Sharing both vulnerabilities and successes and offering support to others can help turn casual acquaintances into meaningful allies in your network.

Reciprocity forms the bedrock of any nurturing network, creating a harmonious exchange where you give as much as you receive. This balance ensures that every member feels valued and acknowledged. Engaging in acts of kindness—whether offering a listening ear during tough times, sharing resources, or giving supportive feedback—is crucial for sustaining the network. Fostering a culture of mutual generosity and support enriches the community and ensures its longevity. While you may derive fulfillment from supporting others, it's vital to also allow yourself to receive support. Healthy relationships thrive on a balance of giving and receiving, maintaining the vitality and reciprocity of your connections.

Self-love and self-worth are essential for forming and nurturing supportive networks. When you value yourself, you naturally gravitate towards relationships that mirror this respect and appreciation. Self-love empowers you to seek out and cultivate connections with people who uplift and encourage you, fostering a network that aligns with your values and aspirations. By prioritizing self-love, you create a filter that helps you choose relationships that genuinely enhance your personal growth and well-being. This foundation strengthens your ability to contribute positively to others and to receive support in return, cultivating a network that sustains and enriches both you and those within it.

As you reflect on the relationships in your life, consider the roles they play. Do they bring you joy and contribute to your growth, or do they leave you feeling drained and diminished? Supportive networks have a unique ability to bring out the best in everyone involved. They go beyond providing support; they also encourage each member to be a pillar of strength, creating a harmonious balance of giving and receiving. As you nurture these relationships, you'll discover that they not only enrich your life but also strengthen the foundation of your journey toward self-love and fulfillment. Each interaction within this network reinforces your sense of worth and supports your personal growth, creating a positive cycle of mutual encouragement and support.

Transitioning to the next chapter, we will explore the external challenges that frequently obstruct our journey to self-love. From societal expectations to personal setbacks, understanding these obstacles will empower us to navigate them effectively. Remember, the strength of your relationships often mirrors the strength within yourself; as you grow personally, your connections also grow. Let's apply the lessons from our supportive networks to confront these challenges with resilience and grace.

# CHAPTER 9

# OVERCOMING EXTERNAL CHALLENGES

*"It's not that I'm so smart, it's just that I stay with problems longer."*
– Albert Einstein

Imagine you're climbing a steep, winding trail. With each step, the path presents new challenges—loose stones, sudden drops, and obscured views. It can be exhausting and disheartening at times, yet invigorating because each obstacle makes you stronger and more adept at navigating. This metaphor mirrors the journey to self-love, especially when external challenges, such as feelings of defeat, appear to block your path forward.

## 9.1 "I've Tried Everything": Addressing Feelings of Defeat

In this part of your adventure, it's not uncommon to feel as though every strategy you've tried has led nowhere. You've read the books, applied the tips, maybe even attended workshops, but the sense of defeat lingers, like a fog that won't lift. Let me tell you, you're not alone in this feeling. It's a shared struggle, one that doesn't highlight failure but rather the complexity of human growth.

### Acknowledging the Struggle

First and foremost, it's crucial to validate these feelings of defeat. They are not signs of failure; rather, they signify the significant and often challenging work you are engaged in. The journey to self-love is marked by setbacks. It's completely normal to feel like you've stumbled or regressed at times. But here's the important perspective—each setback is less about failing and more about learning. It's an integral part of your growth process. Each time you encounter a setback, it's an opportunity to peel back another layer, uncovering more about yourself and how you respond to challenges. And with each rise after a fall, you'll discover that you're a bit stronger, a bit more resilient than before.

### Analyzing Past Efforts

When confronting feelings of defeat, it's beneficial to reflect on past experiences. What strategies have you tried before? What was effective, and what wasn't? Most importantly, why did certain methods work or not work for you? Think of this reflection as a scientific experiment where each attempt provides valuable data. For instance, you might find that journaling didn't quite resonate with you, but meditation brought a sense of peace. Or perhaps group therapy felt overwhelming, whereas one-on-one sessions were deeply insightful. This analysis isn't about criticizing your efforts but understanding how different approaches interact with your unique emotional landscape.

### Adjusting Expectations and Methods

In the journey of self-love, adjusting your expectations is crucial. It's about setting realistic and achievable goals. Rather than aiming to overhaul your self-esteem in a month, consider focusing on smaller, more manageable objectives. Celebrate minor victories—like choosing a healthy meal, saying no when you're overcommitted, or simply acknowledging your emotions without judgment. These small steps accumulate over time and contribute to meaningful, lasting changes.

### Provide Encouragement, Support, and Empathy

Remember, this journey is lifelong. There's no final destination because who you are continues to evolve. So, give yourself the compassion you would offer a good friend. Be gentle with your setbacks and patient with your progress. Celebrate the fact that you're trying, that you're committed to improving your relationship with yourself. That commitment, that courage to keep going even when it's tough, is worth more than you might realize right now. Every step you take is a testament to your growth and resilience.

As you stand on this trail, looking ahead at its twists and turns, remember that every step, every effort, shapes who you are. It's not just about reaching the peak; it's about growing stronger with each small climb. You can do this, not because the path is easy, but because you have the capability to navigate it, no matter how tough it gets. Keep moving forward, keep evolving, and understand that with each step, you're getting closer to becoming the person you want to be.

## 9.2 Navigating Criticism and External Judgments

Criticism, whether from someone close or a mere acquaintance, can feel like a sharp gust of wind, momentarily taking your breath away. It's a common part of being human, but that doesn't make it any easier to handle, especially when it seems to come from all sides: family, friends, coworkers, or societal expectations. Understanding the source of these criticisms can greatly influence how you interpret and respond to them. Often, they reflect more about the giver's own perspectives and biases than your own worth or actions. For example, a family member might criticize your career choices based on their own fears and experiences, while a friend might project their own insecurities onto you regarding life decisions.

Distinguishing between helpful and harmful feedback is crucial for handling outside opinions effectively. Helpful feedback, even if it's a bit painful to hear, is intended to help you improve. It's respectful and usually includes specific suggestions for how you can do better. For instance, if a mentor suggests adding more engaging visuals to your project presentation, they're trying to enhance your skills. On the other hand, harmful feedback lacks support or practical advice. It can make you feel small and discouraged, offering no clear way for you to get better or learn from the experience.

To protect yourself from the negative effects of harsh criticism, it's important to develop emotional resilience. This doesn't mean putting up walls or getting defensive. Instead, it involves strengthening your ability to handle criticism without letting it undermine your self-esteem. One effective technique is cognitive reframing, where you actively choose to interpret feedback in a way that supports your personal growth. For example, if someone says, "Your ideas are too simplistic," you can reframe it as, "I should focus on adding more depth to my ideas. What resources can help me achieve that?" This approach not only reduces the impact of criticism but also turns it into a valuable tool for improvement.

Another empowering strategy is to create a feedback filter. This involves developing a mental process to sift through criticism, keeping what is helpful and disregarding what isn't. Begin by asking yourself a few key questions: Is this feedback valid? Is its intention to help me improve? Does it align with my values and goals? If the answers are affirmative, consider integrating the feedback into your plans for improvement. If not, it's best to let it go. This selective approach ensures you remain focused on growth opportunities that come from genuine, constructive feedback, without being weighed down by every critique.

Handling criticism and external judgments is like navigating through challenging waters—steadfastly maintaining your course even when faced with adversity. It involves listening carefully, refining your approach, and at times, choosing to go against the prevailing opinion because you believe strongly in your chosen direction. It's important to note that the goal isn't to become immune to criticism, but rather to develop a relationship with feedback that strengthens and enhances both your personal and professional life. By understanding the source of feedback, identifying its constructive or destructive nature, and employing tools such as cognitive reframing and a reliable feedback filter, you can embrace criticism as a valuable ally in your journey toward growth and self-improvement.

## 9.3 Dealing with Setbacks and Failures

Setbacks and failures often feel deeply personal, like harsh judgments of our abilities. But what if we looked at them differently? What if, instead of signs of our shortcomings, we saw them as integral parts of a richer human experience? The fear of rejection and failure is widespread, often stemming from early experiences where failure led to disappointment or disapproval. This fear can create barriers not only to success but also to attempting anything where failure is a possibility. It's important to recognize that these fears are common and affect people across various settings, from classrooms to boardrooms. Acknowledging this reality can significantly reduce their power over us.

It's crucial to reframe how we perceive setbacks and failures. Instead of seeing them as catastrophes, we can view them as inevitable steps toward gaining deeper understanding and mastery. Every inventor, artist, and pioneer has encountered numerous setbacks and failures on their journey to success. What sets them apart isn't a flawless track record, but their resilience to persevere despite setbacks. Oprah Winfrey was fired from her first job as a news anchor, Steve Jobs was fired from Apple in 1985, JK Rowling's Harry Potter was rejected by 30 publishers, Colonel Sanders was rejected by over 1,000 restaurants before establishing KFC, Tomas Eddison failed 1,000 times before perfecting the light bulb, the Wright Brothers were told it was impossible to create a flying machine and Micheal Jordan was cut from his high school basketball team. When we start to regard setbacks as normal and essential parts of the learning process, much of the fear and stigma surrounding failure dissipates. This shift in perspective is freeing, enabling us to take risks and push boundaries without being paralyzed by the fear of failure.

Learning from failures is just as crucial as changing how we perceive them. When faced with a setback, instead of criticizing yourself, ask, "What can I learn from this?" This mindset transforms a negative experience into a valuable lesson that can inform future endeavors. For example, if a work project doesn't achieve the desired outcomes, take time to evaluate the process. What went awry, and why? How could things be approached differently next time? This analysis isn't about placing blame, but rather about gathering insights that can lead to improvement. By methodically examining our failures, we construct a roadmap for future success, armed with the wisdom gained from past mistakes.

Staying motivated in the face of setbacks requires a strategic approach. It's normal to feel discouraged after a setback, but taking a broader view of the situation can be beneficial. Setting short-term, achievable goals can serve as stepping stones to rebuild confidence gradually. For instance, if a job application doesn't pan out, a recovery goal could be to update your CV or acquire a new skill relevant to your field within the next two weeks. Alongside personal milestones, drawing support from mentors, colleagues, or friends can provide a crucial support network. Sharing your challenges and vulnerabilities with empathetic individuals can significantly ease your emotional burden and reignite your motivation.

Finally, celebrating your efforts regardless of outcomes fosters a positive attitude towards risk-taking. By rewarding yourself for your efforts, regardless of the results, you cultivate a sense of self-worth that isn't solely dependent on external achievements. This practice promotes a more adventurous and open approach to life and its challenges. It's important to remember that you're human, and imperfection is a natural part of being human. Embracing this reality can transform how you navigate life's inevitable ups and downs.

So, the next time you encounter a setback, pause to breathe and reflect. Each misstep isn't a step backward but rather a step forward in its own way, providing valuable insights and opportunities that guide you toward your goals.

# 9.4 Balancing Ambition with Self-Care

In the whirlwind of daily responsibilities and ambitions, it's easy to find yourself rushing from one task to the next, striving for excellence in every aspect of your life. Many people, especially those who haven't fully embraced self-care, tend to push themselves to the limits at work or in personal pursuits, often neglecting their own well-being. You might constantly say 'yes' to every request, stay late at work regularly, or take on additional projects even when you're already overwhelmed. While ambition is commendable, when it begins to overshadow your need for self-care, it's crucial to pause and reassess.

### *Identifying Signs of Imbalance*

The first step to regain balance is recognizing the signs that your drive to achieve may be taking a toll on you. One clear indicator is chronic stress. If you often feel tense, find it hard to relax, or are constantly worried about work, it's a sign that your work-life balance needs attention. Another sign is neglecting personal needs—like skipping meals, sacrificing sleep, or skipping exercise because of external demands. Strained relationships can also be a warning sign. If loved ones mention missing time with you, or if you feel too drained for social activities, it's important to reassess your priorities.

### *Set Boundaries for Work-Life Balance*

Establishing clear boundaries is essential for balancing your ambitions with personal well-being. Start by clearly defining and communicating your limits, especially in your work environment. For example, let your colleagues or clients know that you won't check emails after 6 PM or on weekends, except for emergencies.

Initially, setting these boundaries may feel challenging, especially if you're used to always being available. It requires a strong commitment to your own health and an understanding that saying no to others can be a positive step for your well-being. It's common to worry that setting boundaries could lead to negative outcomes, like losing your job. However, observing your workplace might show that others are already practicing this balance without issues. The key is in how you approach it. By actively defining and communicating your boundaries, you advocate for your own needs. If the workload becomes overwhelming, it's the organization's responsibility to provide adequate support or resources, rather than expecting you to handle everything alone.

### Setting Sustainable Goals

When setting your professional goals, it's crucial that they are not only achievable but also deeply aligned with your core values. This alignment forms the foundation of genuine fulfillment, going beyond mere accomplishment. For instance, if lifelong learning is important to you, strive to attend workshops or complete courses in your field regularly. Avoid pursuing overly ambitious goals, such as obtaining another degree solely for resume enhancement, especially if it doesn't contribute to your growth or align with your long-term aspirations. Such pursuits, while impressive on paper, can detract from your well-being by prioritizing external recognition over internal satisfaction. By ensuring your ambitions reflect what truly matters to you, you create a career path that not only leads to success but also nurtures your personal development and happiness.

## *Integrating Self-Care into the Workday*

Incorporating self-care into your daily routine doesn't need to be time-consuming; it can be as simple as taking scheduled breaks during your workday to step outside, meditate, or do some stretches. Another effective practice is mindful eating—taking the time to enjoy your lunch without distractions like emails or work calls. These small habits can greatly enhance your mental and physical energy, making you more productive and content.

## *Reassessing Priorities Regularly*

Life's constant flux mirrors the evolution of your needs and ambitions. Continuously assessing what truly matters to you helps maintain focus on what genuinely enriches your life, rather than just enhancing your resume. This process may involve analyzing your current tasks, the projects you're involved in, or reevaluating your career path. Opting for paths that align with your well-being rather than solely your professional profile is crucial. If you find that your commitments are more draining than fulfilling, it might be a sign to let go of some responsibilities or pursue opportunities that better suit your life's rhythm. Initially, advocating for your needs and declining additional tasks can feel challenging. However, with practice, this self-advocacy becomes a more natural and empowering part of your routine.

In navigating these adjustments, remember that your well-being is not a luxury but a necessity. Balancing ambition with self-care isn't about compromising your goals; it's about ensuring that your journey toward them is healthy and sustainable. By establishing clear boundaries, aligning your goals with your values, incorporating self-care into your daily routine, and regularly reevaluating your priorities, you create a life that supports both your achievements and your happiness. This balance isn't just beneficial for you; it also allows you to bring your best self to every aspect of your life, benefiting those around you as well.

## 9.5 Harnessing Resilience and Turning Obstacles into Opportunities

My grandmother's life story is a testament to resilience. At just seven years old, after her mother's death from an autoimmune disease and pneumonia, she stepped into a caretaking role within her family. With her father battling alcoholism and often absent, she took on responsibilities like tending to animals on their farm early each morning and getting her brother up and ready for school each day. Despite these early challenges, she persevered, finding strength and direction in her faith. Her journey was marked by hardships, including the loss of her first child and a personal battle with a debilitating autoimmune disease, for which treatments were limited during her time. Yet, she never wavered in her dedication to her family, managing severe pain and fatigue while raising her two daughters and fulfilling her work commitments. Whenever I asked her how she kept pushing forward despite such adversity, her answer was always simple yet profound: "There's no other option. You just have to keep moving forward." Recently, she faced the loss of her lifelong companion, her husband, whom she had known since she was six years old. Despite the depth of her grief, her determination remains strong, often saying, "I'll be okay. I've still got a lot of life to live." Her unwavering spirit and refusal to see herself as a victim are what define her strength. Through her example, and the stories of many others who have overcome significant challenges, we are reminded of the power of our own inner resilience. It's a reminder to embrace resilience and to commit, each day, to living our best lives, knowing we have only one life to live.

Resilience transcends mere recovery from setbacks. It's the artful skill of navigating through storms, where each raindrop contributes to your journey of empowerment and fortitude. This concept exemplifies one of my favorite quotes, "Life isn't about waiting for the storm to pass, it's about learning to dance in the rain." Resilience encompasses the remarkable ability to confront adversities and transform them into catalysts for personal growth. It's cultivated through a blend of persistence and ingenuity, empowering you to face life's challenges with grace and resilience.

Developing resilience starts with recognizing that stress and obstacles are not barriers but integral aspects of life's landscape. When I reflect on resilience, I'm reminded of a resilient flower pushing through tough concrete or a tree majestically growing from a craggy cliff. Despite their challenging environments, they thrive, becoming beautiful examples of nature's determination. Similarly, the Japanese art of Kintsugi, where broken pottery is repaired with gold, serves as a metaphor for our lives. It teaches us that our trials and tribulations are not mere setbacks but essential parts of our journey, shaping who we are. They are the golden seams of our existence. While challenges may temporarily disrupt us, embracing resilience allows us to rebuild ourselves into stronger, more refined individuals. Through resilience, each obstacle we overcome enriches the tapestry of our lives, transforming us into symbols of resilience and inner beauty.

Harnessing resilience and transforming obstacles into opportunities is about more than mere survival; it's about thriving. It involves taking life's challenges and weaving them into chapters of your success story. As you cultivate resilience, remember that each obstacle you face and conquer showcases your strength and adaptability. This approach isn't just about preparing yourself for future challenges; it's about using them as catalysts for growth and self-discovery. As we conclude this exploration of resilience, carry forward the understanding that the obstacles you encounter aren't mere hurdles to clear. They are opportunities to deepen your strength, enrich your experiences, and continue on your journey of personal growth.

# CHAPTER 10

# LIFE TRANSITIONS AND SELF-LOVE

*"Our very survival depends on our ability to stay awake, to adjust to new ideas, to remain vigilant and to face the challenge of change."*
– Martin Luther King Jr.

As we move through life, from childhood to adulthood, and later into parenthood and senior years, we experience significant changes. For women, these transitions often mean taking on caregiving roles—as a partner, mother, or even grandmother—each bringing its own joys and challenges. As we age, our bodies change, and menopause brings further physical, emotional, and societal adjustments. Embracing these changes with self-love and grace allows us to thrive in every stage of life.

## 10.1 Navigating the Waters of Young Adulthood and Marriage

Young adulthood is often marked by the pursuit of independence, self-discovery, and exploring romantic relationships. For young women, this time is crucial for developing self-love, which forms a strong foundation for self-worth and fulfilling relationships. Embracing self-love means recognizing your inherent value, setting clear personal boundaries, and actively pursuing your dreams and goals. This phase is vital for introspection and self-appreciation. It's important not to rush into romantic relationships to fill internal voids of love. Instead, focus on building your own emotional well-being before including a partner in your life journey.

As we enter marriage or long-term partnerships, the importance of self-love only grows. In marriage, self-love helps us maintain our individuality, advocate for our needs, and communicate openly and honestly. It empowers us to create a partnership where both partners feel valued, understood, and supported. Developing self-love as a young single adult and continuing to nurture it in marriage ensures a journey of growth, mutual respect, and deep, lasting love.

Navigating the transition into marriage or long-term partnerships, it's crucial not to lose yourself while caring for your partner. Prioritizing their happiness at the expense of your own well-being can harm the relationship over time. A healthy partnership is balanced, with both giving and receiving. This is not just physical, but emotional as well, allowing yourself to speak up and share your feelings when necessary. Ensuring that nurturing your partner doesn't overshadow caring for yourself, and continuing to pursue your own interests and desires, is essential for a harmonious and lasting relationship.

## 10.2 Navigating Self-Love as a Parent

When you first hold your child, the world changes. Suddenly, there's this tiny being whose needs seem to come before your own. As a mom, it's easy to put everything on hold for your kids, falling into a routine where your own needs are always on the back burner. While this sacrificial love is noble, it can make you forget the essential person in this equation—

you. Remember, caring for yourself is not a luxury but a necessity. Taking care of yourself enables you to be there for your children in the best way possible.

Parenting comes with many pressures and challenges, from managing daily logistics to the emotional labor of nurturing a child's growth. This can deplete your emotional and physical reserves if not balanced with self-care. For moms, this imbalance can show up in subtle ways—you might stop engaging in activities you once loved or feel constantly tired and irritable. Remember, self-care isn't selfish; it's the foundation that supports your family's well-being. Even small self-care actions, like taking fifteen minutes to read a book, practice yoga, or sit quietly with a cup of tea, can significantly improve your energy and perspective.

Promoting self-compassion in parenting means setting realistic expectations for yourself and forgiving your imperfections. Parenting isn't about perfection; it's a beautifully messy part of life where mistakes are inevitable. Embracing imperfection can relieve unnecessary pressure. Acknowledge that it's okay not to have all the answers and to feel overwhelmed sometimes. Give yourself the same grace you offer your children, recognizing that you are doing your best with the resources you have. This mindset fosters a healthier emotional environment for you and teaches your children important lessons in self-compassion.

Maintaining your identity beyond being a parent is essential for nurturing self-love. It's easy to lose yourself in the demands of parenthood, but reconnecting with your interests and passions can rejuvenate your spirit and enhance your overall satisfaction. Whether returning to a hobby you set aside or exploring new interests, these activities offer a joyful escape and remind you of your individuality outside your parental role. They also provide opportunities for personal growth and can introduce you to communities of like-minded individuals who share your interests.

Speaking of communities, building supportive networks with other parents can be incredibly enriching. These connections offer a platform for sharing experiences and challenges, providing both support and understanding. It's immensely reassuring to discover that other parents share similar struggles and that you're not alone in your feelings. These networks can be found in parenting groups, school associations, or online communities. The key is to engage actively, allowing yourself to both give and receive support. These relationships can significantly boost your emotional resilience and provide practical insights and resources for navigating the complexities of parenthood.

By integrating self-care, self-compassion, personal identity, and supportive networks into your life, you weave a tapestry of self-love that enriches both your own life and deeply benefits your children. Your example demonstrates the importance of loving and valuing oneself. It teaches them that self-care and personal fulfillment are vital components of a well-rounded, happy life, not optional extras. As you explore these aspects of self-love, each step you take in nurturing yourself contributes to a richer, more fulfilling life for both you and your children.

## 10.3 Self-Love in Aging: Embracing the Golden Years

When contemplating aging, what comes to mind? Is it just the physical signs or also the wealth of experience, wisdom, and potential freedom that accompany it? As women, our journey through aging is deeply influenced by our self-perception and the societal narratives we've absorbed. Menopause, for example, is often portrayed as a daunting milestone, marked by difficult physical changes. Symptoms like hot flashes and mood swings can make you feel disconnected from your own body. But here's something empowering: much of this transformation is natural. While challenging, it also signifies a phase of life ripe with opportunities for personal growth and deeper self-awareness.

Accepting these changes often means redefining our relationship with our bodies and ourselves. It's about changing the narrative from loss to transformation. This doesn't mean ignoring the challenges but rather facing them with a mindset of care and compassion instead of criticism and fear. For example, recognizing that hormonal changes are a natural part of aging and addressing symptoms with medical guidance and lifestyle adjustments can turn what might seem disempowering into an opportunity for proactive self-care.

Promoting positive aging is another essential element of self-love during the golden years. Staying active, both mentally and physically, is key to this endeavor. Engaging in activities that stimulate both the mind and body can greatly enhance quality of life. Whether it's joining a dance class, exploring a new hobby, or volunteering in your community, these activities offer more than just a way to pass the time; they provide purpose, joy, and a sense of community. They reinforce the idea that growth and enjoyment are not exclusive to youth but are accessible and crucial at every stage of life.

Addressing ageism and its effects on self-image is crucial. Internalized ageism can make you underestimate your worth or abilities solely based on age. To counteract these stereotypes, begin by acknowledging and questioning them—both in your self-perception and interactions with others. Celebrating your age, embracing your life experiences, and carrying yourself with confidence are revolutionary acts of self-love. They set a strong example not only for your peers but also for younger generations, reshaping societal norms and expanding perspectives on aging.

Engaging in these practices cultivates a profound sense of self-love that enriches your present and brightens your future. It's about redefining aging as a time of vibrant self-discovery and fulfillment. As you journey through these years, remember that aging isn't merely about time passing, but about gathering experiences, wisdom, and an expanding capacity for love—beginning with love for yourself.

## 10.4 Self-Love and Chronic Illness: Strategies for Coping

When life suddenly changes from active and energetic to being dictated by a chronic illness, it can feel like a heavy blanket over your world. The vibrancy dims, and activities that once filled your days may now feel like distant memories. It's a profound shift that brings waves of grief and mourning for the life and abilities once taken for granted. I've been there—tears marking the pages of my own story as I struggled to reconcile who I was with the new limitations my body imposed. But here's what I learned through those dark times: your essence isn't diminished by your physical condition. You are not defined by what you can or cannot do. This realization isn't the end; it's the beginning of adapting and thriving, even within the boundaries set by illness.

Navigating the impact of chronic illness on your self-image and self-esteem requires a compassionate reassessment of what self-love means under these new circumstances. It's common to experience negative self-talk, especially on days when your body feels like an adversary. The inner dialogue may whisper that you are inadequate, not enough, or no longer valuable. It's crucial to confront these thoughts with kindness and counter them with truths rooted in your inherent worth. Affirmations can be a powerful tool in this journey. Simple statements like "I am valuable, regardless of my physical abilities," or "My worth transcends my health," serve as gentle reminders of your unchanging value. These affirmations aren't just words; they are affirmations of truth that need to be embraced daily.

Adaptive self-care routines are essential for managing life with a chronic illness. While self-care is often seen as a luxury, for those coping with illness, it's a vital foundation of daily life. It involves understanding and respecting your new limits and finding ways to nurture your body without pushing beyond its boundaries. This might mean adjusting your expectations of productivity, prioritizing rest when needed, or discovering new hobbies that suit your energy levels. If mobility aids such as wheelchairs or scooters become necessary, embrace them with pride. These tools aren't signs of defeat but instruments that enhance independence and engagement with life.

Accepting your condition doesn't equate to giving up hope or halting the pursuit of happiness; instead, it involves adapting your strategies and discovering new sources of joy. This process may include small adjustments, such as savoring a sunny morning by a window when going outside feels challenging, or larger ones, like redesigning your living environment for better accessibility. This acceptance is fluid and ongoing, requiring continual adjustment as your condition evolves. It's about finding peace with the present—not as surrender, but as a deliberate approach to living your best life possible right now.

The role of community and support is crucial when living with chronic illness. It can often feel isolating, like navigating a solitary journey where few truly grasp the challenges you face. Establishing a network of support—whether through healthcare providers who collaborate in your care, support groups that understand your daily struggles, or loved ones who offer both emotional support and practical assistance—is invaluable. These connections provide not only comfort but also practical advice and solutions that can simplify managing your condition. They serve as a reminder that while your illness may be a part of your life, it doesn't define your entire existence. There's a wealth of experiences still within reach, shared with caring individuals who genuinely understand and support you.

In embracing these strategies, it's important to recognize that adapting to life with a chronic illness showcases resilience. It's a testament to your inner strength and your dedication to living life to the fullest, despite the challenges. Each day you prioritize self-love and self-care, you affirm that your life, though altered, remains profoundly valuable.

## 10.5 Self-Love and Spirituality: Exploring the Connection

Spirituality often defies rigid definitions, yet it undeniably plays a significant role in many people's lives, shaping their values, beliefs, and their sense of connection to the world. In the context of self-love, spirituality can be seen as a broad way to perceive and relate to the essence of who you are beyond physical and mental limitations. It involves connecting with something greater—whether that's a higher power, the universe, nature, or your own soul—and acknowledging the inherent worth and purpose within yourself. This deeper connection cultivates a profound sense of love and self-acceptance, nurturing an inner sanctuary where strength and compassion can thrive.

Incorporating spiritual practices into your daily routine can greatly enrich this connection, with each practice offering a distinct path to inner peace and self-discovery. Meditation, for instance, enables you to quiet the mind and connect deeply with your inner self. It creates a space where you can observe your thoughts and emotions without judgment, gaining a deeper understanding of your inner world and the external influences affecting it. Prayer, regardless of religious background, serves as a direct channel to express gratitude, seek guidance, and reaffirm your intentions. It assists in aligning your daily actions with your spiritual beliefs, fostering a sense of connection to something greater than yourself.

Nature walks and other outdoor activities can be profoundly grounding and uplifting, providing a tangible link to the natural world and reminding us of the cycles and rhythms of life we are all interconnected with. These moments of connection help to contextualize personal challenges, highlighting the beauty and continuity of life while reinforcing our role within it. Rituals also play a crucial role in spiritual practice. Whether they involve daily affirmations, weekly community gatherings, or personal acts such as lighting candles or incense, rituals serve to strengthen our spiritual values. They create regular touchpoints that remind us of our journey and personal growth, offering stability and reaffirmation of our beliefs.

Spirituality offers profound healing benefits. Engaging in spiritual practices can bring comfort in times of difficulty, offering stability and fostering hope. Practices like forgiveness and acceptance, central to many spiritual traditions, serve as powerful tools for emotional healing.

Forgiveness, both of oneself and others, lightens the emotional load we carry, creating room for new growth and experiences. It releases burdens that may have been held onto for too long, promoting inner peace and healing. Acceptance plays a complementary role by allowing us to embrace life as it unfolds. It encourages us to find contentment in the present moment, free from harsh self-judgment or unrealistic expectations, fostering a sense of peace and gratitude.

I encourage you to explore your own spiritual beliefs and practices, discovering how they can enrich your daily life and support your journey toward self-love. This exploration is deeply personal and can vary widely among individuals. You might find resonance in reading spiritual texts, connecting with communities that share your values, or dedicating time each day to quiet reflection. The essence lies in selecting practices that feel meaningful and nurturing to you, fostering personal growth and aligning with your unique perspective on life. Embrace what resonates most deeply within you as you cultivate a deeper spiritual connection that supports your path to self-love.

As you incorporate spiritual practices into your life, you may discover that they not only enrich your relationship with yourself but also deepen your connections with others. Shared spiritual experiences can be profoundly impactful, creating a sense of community and mutual understanding that goes beyond everyday interactions. They serve as reminders that we are not alone in our challenges or our moments of happiness and that our journey is intertwined in meaningful ways with those around us.

In conclusion, spirituality and self-love intertwine deeply, each enhancing the other in ways that can profoundly impact your well being and perspective on life. By embracing and integrating your spiritual beliefs and practices into your daily life, you establish a strong foundation for personal growth and develop a deeper, more compassionate relationship with yourself. This chapter has explored how this connection can manifest and support you on your journey toward greater self-love and fulfillment. Moving forward, each step in this exploration leads toward a more grounded, peaceful, and loving existence.

# CHAPTER 11

# DAILY PRACTICES FOR SELF-EMPOWERMENT

*"Every day do something that will inch*
*you closer to a better tomorrow."*
– Doug Firebaugh

Imagine this: you're on the edge of a diving board, your toes gripping the edge as you gaze into the deep blue of the pool below. It's a bit daunting, isn't it? Taking that plunge is challenging, yet it marks the beginning of something magical. This chapter encourages you to embrace that leap each day—not into water, but into practices that empower and nourish your inner strength.

## 11.1 Lean Into the Discomfort and Embrace Change

Let's discuss discomfort—not the type you should disregard, like a severe headache or a sprained ankle, but the kind that stirs within, urging you toward growth. It's the discomfort that arises when you're about to tackle something that tests you, whether it's speaking up in a meeting, seeking assistance, or establishing a boundary.

You know that flutter in your stomach? It's more than just nerves; it's your body signaling, "Hey, something significant is unfolding!" It's a sign that you're venturing beyond your comfort zone, where personal growth thrives. Embracing that discomfort each time strengthens your emotional, mental, and spiritual resilience.

## Listening to Your Body and Mind

Being mindful of your body and mind can offer valuable insights into how you navigate and respond to various situations. For example, observe your physical reactions when you feel uneasy. Does your heart race? Do your palms become sweaty? These sensations are cues worth noting because they can help you better understand and regulate your responses.

Similarly, pay attention to your emotions. What feelings arise when you're uncomfortable? Are you scared, excited, or perhaps a blend of both? Identifying these emotions can clarify them and lessen their impact, empowering you to manage them more skillfully and harness them to your benefit.

## Digging Deeper into Discomfort

Understanding why you feel uncomfortable can change it from a vague feeling into a clear call to action. Ask yourself: What exactly is causing this discomfort? Is it fear of failure, fear of judgment, or maybe fear of not meeting high standards? Pinpointing these underlying fears and beliefs that drive your discomfort empowers you to confront them head-on.

For instance, if you discover that your discomfort with public speaking stems from a fear of judgment, you can begin to work on accepting that judgment is a natural aspect of life and that others' opinions don't determine your value. This realization can free you, transforming a challenging experience into an empowering opportunity.

### *Using Discomfort as a Catalyst for Change*

Now, how do you translate this newfound understanding into action? You set intentional, clear, and actionable goals. Building on what you've learned about your discomfort and its origins, set goals that push these boundaries, similar to our discussion on building self-confidence. For instance, if you're uneasy about public speaking, your goal could be to speak up at least once in every meeting. If asking for help makes you apprehensive, challenge yourself to reach out when you encounter difficulties with a task.

Remember, these goals aren't solely about accomplishing external successes; they're about fostering internal growth. They aim to expand your comfort zone incrementally, transforming what once seemed daunting into something manageable, and perhaps even enjoyable. This journey isn't just about confronting fears; it's about reshaping your belief in what you can achieve.

By embracing discomfort, listening to your body's signals, understanding its roots, and setting specific goals, you can turn discomfort from a barrier into a stepping stone. This chapter isn't just about managing discomfort—it's about using it as a potent tool for personal growth and empowerment. As you engage in these practices, you'll discover that you not only become more resilient but also increase your ability to tackle challenges. This is the core of self-empowerment: transforming what intimidates us into what fortifies us.

## 11.2 The 10-Minute Self-Love Practice (ME TIME)

There is an incredible amount of power that can come from setting aside time to spend with yourself. It's exclusively yours—a brief moment dedicated to nurturing your well-being. Welcome to "Me Time," a daily 10-minute ritual crafted to recharge and center you, regardless of your schedule. Consider it a mini-retreat you can indulge in without leaving your space.

Let's outline this nurturing routine into a sequence that fits neatly into a ten-minute timeframe, ensuring it's both manageable and beneficial. Begin with a minute of deep breathing exercises. Find a comfortable seated position, close your eyes, and concentrate on your breath. Inhale deeply through your nose, feeling your chest and belly expand, then exhale slowly through your mouth. This focused breathing lowers stress and centers your mind, setting the stage for the next part of your session.

Next, allocate three minutes to affirmations. These are positive statements that empower you and counteract negative thoughts, fostering a positive self-image. Select affirmations that align with your current emotions or aspirations. Examples include "I am capable of achieving great things" or "I accept myself unconditionally today." Repeat these affirmations aloud with conviction. If you prefer, write them down in a journal if speaking aloud isn't suitable in your current environment.

Moving on, dedicate the next four minutes to journaling your thoughts or expressing gratitude. It doesn't need to be extensive—just a few bullet points will suffice. Reflect on what you're thankful for today and what accomplishments you're proud of. This practice of gratitude shifts your focus from scarcity to abundance in your life, promoting positivity and contentment.

Lastly, use the final two minutes for quiet reflection. Simply allow yourself to 'be'. You can contemplate the affirmations you've repeated, review your journal entries, or simply let your thoughts drift. This time is for connecting with yourself, listening to your inner thoughts and feelings without any judgment.

This routine is meant to be flexible and adaptable. If you're in a busy office, your deep breathing might be more subtle, or you might use a digital app for journaling. The important thing is to tailor it to fit your life and daily needs, rather than forcing yourself to conform to a rigid structure. The beauty of this practice lies in its simplicity and the profound effect it can have on your mental and emotional well-being. Just ten minutes a day dedicated to this routine can greatly enhance your mindfulness, decrease stress, and uplift your mood.

Consistency is key in this practice. Incorporating "Me Time" into your daily routine can bring lasting changes in how you view and care for yourself. It's akin to watering a plant; with regular attention, you'll see it flourish. Over time, this dedicated practice deepens your connection with yourself, cultivating more peace, self-acceptance, and joy. You'll come to appreciate that these ten minutes hold the potential to positively influence the remaining 1,440 minutes of your day. Some days, this small change can make a world of difference.

## 11.3 Journaling for Self-Discovery and Reflection

Journaling is like engaging in a profound conversation with yourself—one that can bring about deep insights and personal growth. It's a tool that helps you clarify your thoughts, track your journey, and uncover patterns in your behavior that may be hindering or advancing you.

Journaling is a transformative practice for delving into the intricacies of your personal story. It aids in unraveling the intricate web of emotions and thoughts woven by daily life. When you express your fears and aspirations on paper, you're not merely documenting events; you're unpacking them. This process sheds light on how specific experiences influence your emotions and actions, offering clarity to make informed decisions and embrace your true self.

Journaling encompasses various techniques, each with its own purpose, yet all aimed at deepening self-awareness and self-compassion. Gratitude journaling, for example, redirects your attention from scarcity to abundance. By consistently recording things you're thankful for, you nurture a mindset of richness and optimism. This habit can markedly uplift your mood and widen your outlook, particularly during difficult times.

Stream of consciousness journaling is another potent technique. It entails jotting down your thoughts as they arise, without concern for structure or punctuation. It's like clearing out mental clutter. This approach can be especially revealing, uncovering your deepest thoughts and emotions, some of which may surprise you as they often remain hidden amidst the busyness of structured daily routines.

Problem-solving journaling is a structured approach that centers on tackling a particular issue or decision by exploring various solutions. Begin by outlining the problem in detail, then brainstorm potential strategies to address it. Evaluate the advantages and disadvantages of each solution, and assess how each option aligns with your values and long-term objectives. This method not only aids in resolving specific issues but also strengthens your decision-making abilities progressively.

To integrate journaling into your daily routine, select a time when you can enjoy uninterrupted personal time. Early mornings or late evenings are often ideal, offering a peaceful moment for reflection and writing. Establishing a conducive environment is also important. Consider lighting a candle, playing soothing music, or sitting by a window with a calming view. The goal is to make this experience enjoyable and comforting, transforming it into a ritual that you anticipate and cherish.

Deepen your self-reflection by utilizing prompts that encourage contemplation of your values, fears, dreams, and significant life events. Questions such as, "Which values hold the most significance for me, and why?" or "What am I most fearful of, and what actions can I take to confront this fear?" foster introspection and personal growth. Reflecting on pivotal life experiences and their influence on your journey can also offer insights into your resilience and capacity to adapt, essential aspects of cultivating self-compassion.

Through these practices, journaling evolves beyond mere record-keeping into a dynamic tool for personal growth and empowerment. It assists you in navigating life's complexities with heightened awareness and confidence. Each page you fill not only chronicles your journey but also strengthens your self-connection, fostering a deeper understanding and appreciation of your present self and aspirations. As you explore and reflect, let your journal serve as a mirror reflecting your authentic self, guiding you through the intricate path of personal growth with honesty and grace.

## 11.4 Cultivating Joy & Gratitude

There's a saying that expressing gratitude is like reaching for the heavens. Embracing this perspective turns even ordinary days into moments filled with wonder and happiness. Establishing a daily gratitude practice goes beyond simply acknowledging life's blessings; it cultivates a mindset that actively attracts positivity and joy.

Keeping a gratitude journal is a profoundly transformative yet beautifully simple practice. Each night, before bed, write down three things that brought you joy or that you're grateful for. These don't have to be big events; often, the smallest observations have the greatest impact. Maybe you're thankful for the delicious taste of your morning coffee, completing a work project, or simply stealing quiet moments for yourself during a hectic day. This habit tunes your mind to appreciate the good things, uplifting your mood and reducing the impact of daily stressors.

Sharing gratitude with loved ones can amplify its benefits, creating a positive feedback loop among friends and family. This practice fosters an environment where joy and thankfulness flow continuously. Try incorporating it into dinner conversations, where each person shares one thing they're grateful for from their day. This habit not only enhances your personal well-being but also strengthens relationships by emphasizing positive interactions.

Now, let's talk about finding joy in the little things. It's easy to overlook the small pleasures of daily life, especially when busy schedules and responsibilities cloud our view. But imagine capturing those fleeting moments of happiness and holding onto them a little longer. This is where mindfulness becomes incredibly powerful. Techniques like mindful eating, walking, or listening can open the door to this practice. For instance, when eating, focus fully on the flavors, textures, and smells of your food. When walking, notice the sensation of the ground under your feet, the sounds of the environment, and the feel of the air on your skin. By being fully present, you allow yourself to truly experience and savor these moments, transforming mundane activities into sources of joy and relaxation.

Through these practices, cultivating joy and gratitude becomes more than just an exercise; it becomes a way of living. Each act and each moment spent in mindful appreciation adds up to a life more vividly lived and deeply felt. As you continue to weave these practices into the fabric of your daily life, watch as your world transforms, colored by the rich hues of joy and the warm light of gratitude.

## 11.5 Meditation and Mindfulness for Inner Peace

Several years ago, when my mom and younger brother were dropping me off at college, marking my first venture into living independently, the air was thick with a mix of excitement and nostalgia. In an attempt to inject some light-heartedness into our farewells, I recalled a humorous saying from a friend. Turning to my brother, I quipped, "Just always remember, Bud, wherever you go, there you are." The simplicity and humor of the statement drew laughter from us all. Years later, my brother gifted me a book for my birthday titled "Wherever You Go, There You Are," reigniting our amusement over the phrase. Yet, as I delved into the book, I discovered its focus on meditation, prompting me to reconsider the phrase's deeper implication. "Wherever you go, there you are" suggests a profound truth often overlooked in our hectic lives. Amidst the flurry of daily activities and the constant barrage of thoughts about the past and future, truly being present in the moment is a rare state. Our minds seldom dwell in calm and relaxation; they rarely spend time in the present. Mindfulness and meditation emerge as vital practices in this context, offering not just a reprieve for our busy minds but also a means to forge a deeper connection with our inner selves and be mentally present. Think about it: "Wherever you go, there you are." But are you really there? Maybe physically, but are you mentally present? These practices are invaluable tools for navigating the turbulent waters of life, providing a sense of peace and clarity that can light our way through challenging times and allow us to truly embrace the precious moments of the life we live.

Meditation is often seen as sitting cross-legged with closed eyes and an empty mind. However, it's much simpler than that. At its core, meditation is about awareness and coming back to it when your mind drifts. It's about watching your thoughts and feelings without judging them, and then gently bringing your focus back to something specific, like your breath, a word, or an image. This practice helps your mind stay focused and present, reducing the mental 'noise' that causes stress.

For beginners, a simple meditation technique is focused breathing. Find a comfortable seat, close your eyes, and take a few deep breaths to settle in. Then, shift your focus to your natural breathing, noticing each inhale and exhale. Thoughts will come up, and that's okay. The key is not to engage with them. Instead, acknowledge them and gently bring your attention back to your breath. This practice can be done for just five minutes a day and is profoundly calming. To learn more about starting meditation, search "meditation for beginners" on YouTube. There are countless helpful videos available.

Guided imagery is another great technique for beginners. It involves visualizing a peaceful scene, like a quiet beach at sunset or a cozy cabin in the woods. As you imagine this place, engage all your senses to make it vivid. What do you hear? How does it smell? What textures are around you? This form of meditation is effective for reducing anxiety and promoting relaxation, as it distracts your mind from current stresses and focuses it on calming thoughts.

Mindfulness takes the principles of meditation into everyday life. It means being aware moment by moment of our thoughts, feelings, bodily sensations, and surroundings. Mindfulness includes acceptance, where we observe our thoughts and feelings without judging them—without thinking there's a 'right' or 'wrong' way to think or feel at any moment.

Regular meditation and mindfulness offer extensive benefits. Psychologically, they can lessen symptoms of anxiety, depression, and stress. They improve mood, enhance emotional stability, and boost cognitive function, including concentration and attention. One of their most significant benefits is the improved ability to manage stress effectively. By becoming more aware of your emotional and physical responses to stress, you can navigate challenging situations more skillfully, making choices that lead to a more balanced and peaceful life.

Incorporating these practices into your daily routine doesn't require big changes. It begins with small, intentional moments where you decide to pause, breathe, and be present. Gradually, these moments establish a foundation of inner peace that enhances your relationship with yourself and improves interactions with others. Whether you're experienced or new to these practices, meditation and mindfulness offer a path to tranquility and self-discovery that can deeply enrich your life.

# | 11.6 Taking Care of Your Body

Until the age of 28, I thrived on an active lifestyle filled with sports, hiking, dancing, and outdoor adventures that brought me immense joy. However, seven years ago, my vibrant life abruptly changed. My immune system began attacking my body, causing debilitating pain and fatigue that made even simple tasks like showering or climbing stairs nearly impossible. Describing the intensity of this fatigue is difficult. I deeply missed the days when I could lace up my running shoes for a morning jog or glide around the lake on rollerblades. The longing to join friends for salsa nights downtown was palpable. They say we often don't appreciate what we have until it's gone.

When I created my Whole Health Transformation Program several years ago, I never imagined that the most important element to individuals' success in improving their overall health and losing weight was self-love. If you came to me wanting to lose weight and I told you that to be successful we need to first work on self-love you would likely roll your eyes and find a different program. I would have too before working with hundreds of women. When we genuinely love ourselves our motivation for being healthy and losing weight reaches far beyond the number on the scale. We can all set goals and have enough willpower to stick to them for a period, but unless we are motivated with genuine love for ourselves and our bodies, our supply of willpower will eventually run dry. When we genuinely love who we are, we strive to care for our bodies, and when we prioritize our well-being, our self-love grows. Thus, taking care of our physical health is an essential component of cultivating self-love.

We will discuss three core principles in caring for your physical health: physical activity, nutrition, and adequate sleep

## *Physical Activity*

It has been said that if the benefits of exercise could be bottled into a pill, it would be worth millions, yet we often take it for granted. Physical activity's true value goes beyond physical health; it's essential for mental well-being and aids in developing self-love. Physical activity triggers the release of chemicals called endorphins in your body. These natural painkillers not only elevate mood and reduce pain but also play a crucial role in alleviating symptoms of depression and anxiety. Think of them as nature's own anti-anxiety and antidepressant, without the side effects.

When it comes to exercise, there's a wide array of options to consider. The best type of exercise is one that you enjoy and can sustain over time. For example, yoga not only enhances physical flexibility and strength but also incorporates breathing exercises and meditation to reduce stress and enhance mental clarity. Cardiovascular activities like running, cycling, or swimming are excellent for improving heart health and increasing endorphin levels. Strength training, such as weightlifting or using resistance bands, builds muscle, boosts metabolism, and can significantly elevate mood by raising levels of endorphins, dopamine, and serotonin.

Incorporating regular exercise into your daily life doesn't need to be overwhelming; it can be as simple as taking a brisk walk around the block or doing a 10-minute home workout. Consistency and enjoyment are key. If you're new to regular exercise, start small—try 5 minutes of physical activity a couple of times a week. Gradually increase the duration and frequency as your stamina and strength improve. This approach helps prevent overwhelm and makes it easier to maintain the habit over time.

## *Nutrition*

Imagine loving yourself so deeply that every decision you make for your body stems from a profound sense of care and respect. This kind of self-love goes beyond emotional and mental well-being; it involves nourishing your body with the nutrients it requires to thrive. When you genuinely value yourself, prioritizing a diet that supports your overall health becomes essential, not just something you consider later on.

The foods we eat play a crucial role in both our physical and mental well-being. It's intriguing, yet not surprising, that the nutrients we consume can impact our brain chemistry and, consequently, our emotions and behaviors. For example, omega-3 fatty acids found in fish like salmon are known to enhance cognitive function and may alleviate symptoms of depression. Conversely, diets high in processed foods and sugars can worsen feelings of anxiety and depression. This connection underscores that our diet not only fuels our bodies but also nourishes our minds, affecting how we feel each day.

Maintaining a balanced diet is crucial. This involves consuming a diverse range of foods that offer essential nutrients to support both physical and mental well-being. Focus on including colorful vegetables and fruits, lean proteins, whole grains, and healthy fats in your meals. Each meal presents a chance to supply your body with the necessary components for energy, recovery, and optimal mental health.

If you're keen on exploring how a balanced, nutrient-packed diet can enhance overall wellness beyond just weight management, consider our 10-week Whole Health Transformation Program. This program is designed to tackle common challenges women encounter in maintaining healthy eating habits amid busy schedules and diverse responsibilities. It offers practical tools and strategies not just for nutritious eating but also for cultivating a sustainable lifestyle that promotes self-care through nourishing choices. For more details, visit our website at www.mywholeandhappylife.com or find further information at the end of this book.

### Adequate Sleep

Consider sleep as your body's closest ally—the one always supporting your recovery, rejuvenation, and energy restoration. It's tempting to cut back on sleep, sacrificing it for late-night emails, another episode of your favorite show, or extra time on social media. But here's the truth: compromising on sleep is like removing the cornerstone from a sturdy tower of wellness practices. Without it, the entire structure becomes unstable. Let's explore why quality sleep is vital, particularly for your mental well-being, and discover how to create an environment that promotes restful nights.

Sleep isn't merely a passive break. It's an active phase for your brain, where crucial processes like memory consolidation, creative associations, toxin removal, and emotional balance take place. It acts as the ultimate multitasker, supporting mental clarity and resilience. Insufficient sleep can lead to irritability, increased stress, and diminished psychological resilience over time, making it harder to handle daily pressures. It also plays a significant role in weight management—lack of sleep can elevate cortisol levels, hindering weight loss efforts and promoting fat retention.

Maintaining a consistent sleep schedule is one of the most effective strategies for promoting sleep health. Going to bed and waking up at the same time each day, including weekends, helps regulate your body's internal clock, known as the circadian rhythm. This regularity strengthens your body's natural sleep-wake cycle, making it easier to fall asleep and wake up without needing an alarm. It's like setting your body's internal alarm clock to a rhythm that aligns with your natural sleep patterns.

Understanding the crucial role sleep plays in your mental and physical well-being, and actively working to achieve restful nights, enhances your overall quality of life. Each night of good sleep contributes to a healthier, happier you, supporting everything from brain function and mood to metabolism and immune system strength. So tonight, when tempted to sacrifice sleep for another episode or email, remember: sleep is not a luxury—it's a fundamental pillar of your health. Prioritizing sleep is investing in your well-being and vitality for the long term.

# CHAPTER 12

# BRINGING IT FULL CIRCLE

*"I may not have gone where I intended to go, but I think
I have ended up where I intended to be."*
– Douglas Adams

## 12.1 My Personal and Professional Journey

At the age of 16, my parents went through a devastating divorce. The ground seemed to crumble beneath me, leaving me to wrestle with feelings of betrayal and abandonment. This pivotal moment marked the start of a journey—not just through my own pain, but toward a deeper discovery of self-love and healing.

Life, as I had known it, felt shattered. Every significant relationship seemed tainted by the turmoil of my parents' divorce. In my search for stability, I immersed myself in academics and extracurricular activities, believing that achieving success could shield me from feelings of inadequacy and heartbreak. This drive led me to pursue a career in pharmacy—a path that offered stability and an opportunity to validate my own value.

As I delved into my pharmacy studies, the emotional baggage I hadn't addressed started to take its toll. The demanding coursework and self-imposed pressure pushed me to my limits. I vividly recall coming home one day after class, completely drained, and collapsing in tears on my bedroom floor. It wasn't just the academic stress; it was everything I had been avoiding—my fears, my losses, and the deep sense of loneliness.

That breakdown became my epiphany. It compelled me to confront the truth that I wasn't okay—that no level of external achievement could heal the wounds I carried. I understood that I had to confront my past, to delve deeply into the emotional turmoil I had been avoiding. This realization marked the beginning of years spent in therapy, dedicated to self-exploration, and, most importantly, the gradual journey of learning to genuinely care for myself.

After years of diligent effort, I began to feel restored. I finished my education and residency, and I achieved my dream job as a pharmacist at the Mayo Clinic. However, life had another challenge in store for me. Just nine months into what I believed was the culmination of my hard work, I started experiencing severe wrist pain. This marked the beginning of an autoimmune disease that eventually left me bedridden and in chronic pain.

During those challenging months confined to my bed, I grappled with a difficult question: What if instead of burying the pain I addressed it and allowed myself to heal? Could I have prevented a lifelong illness? It was during this period of introspection and personal hardship that I came across stories of people like Lady Gaga who had experienced trauma that was left unaddressed and later evolved into PTSD and chronic pain. In sharing about her condition she said, "My pain really does me no good unless I can transform it into something that is." Inspired by their resilience, I resolved to channel my own experiences into creating something meaningful.

My journey through chronic illness taught me that self-love goes beyond feeling good about yourself during good times. It's about how you treat yourself when you're at your lowest. It's about the conversations you have with yourself in the quiet moments of the night, the kind or critical words you use to narrate your own journey. I discovered that genuine self-love requires a continuous dedication to self-care, compassion, and making choices that align with not only who you are now, but who you aspire to be.

This chapter, and indeed this book, extends an invitation to you. It's an invitation to embark on your own voyage of self-discovery and healing. Just as I learned, every challenge and setback harbors the seeds of growth and renewal. As you read these pages and contemplate your own journey, remember that the path to self-love isn't straightforward. It winds through shadows and light, demanding courage to confront yourself—embracing both imperfections and potential alike. The quote at the beginning of this chapter now rings truer than ever, "I may not have gone where I intended to go, but I think I have ended up where I intended to be."

## 12.2 Transforming Pain into Power

Lying in my bed, which had become my confine due to severe fatigue, I grappled with a profound realization—not only about facing physical ailments but also about overcoming life's unexpected hurdles. It dawned on me that genuine health extends beyond the physical body; it encompasses nurturing the mind and spirit as well. This epiphany laid the foundation for something far-reaching: my Whole Health Transformation Program.

Picture entering a sanctuary where every facet of your existence is cared for, where the goal isn't solely about losing weight but about shedding the barriers of doubt, fear, and hesitation that hinder you from fully embracing your potential. This defines the essence of the Whole Health Transformation Program—an environment where transformation originates from within and radiates outward.

When I designed this program, my vision was precise: to provide more than just a conventional health plan or weight loss regimen. I aimed to establish a sanctuary where healing and personal growth unfold across all dimensions—physical, emotional, and mental. This holistic approach distinguishes our program. It's not focused on quick fixes or temporary adjustments; rather, it initiates a profound and sustainable transformation grounded in self-love and comprehensive self-awareness.

The journey unfolds through a structured progression where each stage naturally leads to the next, weaving a path of self-discovery and holistic health. We begin with the Power of Mind where we delve into the intricacies of our brain's biology, gaining deep insight into its mechanisms and motivations. Understanding how our brain functions empowers us to leverage its potential for transformation. This initial phase is pivotal, fostering self-awareness that enriches the entire program and sets the stage for profound personal growth.

Next, we transition into the Power of Growth, inviting a profound exploration of your personal identity. Embracing self-love requires a deep understanding of oneself—recognizing your innate strengths, identifying core values, and envisioning the life you aspire to lead. This journey of self-discovery empowers you to connect with purpose and reveals the unique impact you can have on the world. Through this transformative process, you will cultivate a deeper appreciation for yourself and the love you inherently deserve.

The Power of Awareness comes next. This phase sharpens our focus on the underlying forces shaping our actions. We explore the obstacles that impede our journey toward self-love through engaging activities and reflective exercises. These tools are designed to uncover layers of the psyche and the years of experiences that have shaped and molded it, offering profound insights into motivations and behaviors. They foster a deeper connection with your authentic self, opening the door to reaching your full potential.

In the Power of Self, the journey takes a profound inward turn. Here, the focus shifts to addressing and healing aspects of self-abandonment while nurturing seeds of self-compassion, self-acceptance, and self-appreciation. This phase is crucial for deepening the roots of self-love and fostering a resilient relationship with oneself.

The Power of Knowledge phase represents a transformative exploration into how nutrition and exercise intertwine with your overall health and well-being. Carefully designed, this phase equips you with a deep understanding of how various foods nourish your body, the importance of a well-rounded diet, and how regular physical activity benefits your mental, emotional, and physical state. This stage goes beyond simply following a nutritional plan or workout regimen for health and weight loss. It aims to empower you with insights needed to make choices tailored to your body's unique needs, paving the way for you to achieve both the body and mind of your dreams.

Every part of our program is based on thorough research and evidence from fields like psychology, nutrition, and exercise science. This ensures that all our strategies are proven to support long-term health, weight loss, and well-being. We're honored to have healthcare professionals and renowned experts, including Mayo Clinic Oncologist Harry Fuentes Bayne, MD, MS, participate in our program.

*"I had the pleasure of working with Whitney as my health coach, and I can confidently say that it was one of the most transformative experiences of my life. After going through a challenging divorce, I felt lost and unsure about my future. Emotions overwhelmed me, and I felt disconnected from myself."*

*Having previously tried therapy, I was initially cautious about coaching, fearing it might offer validation rather than true introspection. However, Whitney's program quickly dispelled my concerns. From the start, her professionalism and warm personality stood out. She established a safe, supportive environment where I could freely explore my thoughts and feelings.*

*Her program included insightful exercises that helped me uncover the root causes of my behaviors and address them effectively. What impressed me most was that every teaching was backed by scientific research, making it even more impactful.*

*Whitney's coaching was truly transformative unlike any other self-improvement advice I had encountered before. While I had often heard suggestions to work on myself, Whitney's program provided clear, powerful concepts that shifted my perspective on life.*

*Working with Whitney, I underwent an extraordinary journey of self-discovery that allowed me to reclaim my life. Alongside losing weight and adopting healthier habits, her guidance and support were invaluable to me. I am deeply grateful and eagerly anticipate continuing our work together in the future.*

*Overall, I wholeheartedly recommend Whitney's program to anyone seeking a compassionate, evidence-based approach to self-discovery and personal growth. Thank you, Whitney, for everything!"*

## 12.4 Inspiring Women of Success

As we delve into the transformative journeys of women who have embraced the Whole Health Transformation Program, it's crucial to view these stories not just as testimonials, but as vivid affirmations of how self-love can revolutionize our health and lives. Self-love extends beyond mere acceptance; it shapes a life where every decision reflects deep respect and care for oneself. Here, we celebrate the inspiring stories of women such as Lori, Angie, June, Cindy, and Joyce, highlighting the profound ripple effect of embracing one's journey with an open heart.

Lori's journey began with a familiar scenario—preparing for a major life event and aiming to look and feel her best. Yet, her experience evolved into a profound transformation. When Lori joined us, she sought more than a temporary diet; she desired lasting change beyond a wedding date. We began by comprehensively assessing her body's specific needs, taking into account factors like daily activity levels and menopausal status. This personalized approach enabled us to design a nutrition and fitness regimen focused not only on weight loss but on establishing sustainable health practices.

But Lori's story goes beyond the surface. In our sessions, it became evident that her weight gain was more than just about food—it was tied to unmet emotional needs and unresolved past wounds that manifested in her eating habits. Her relationship with food was intertwined with her personal relationships, especially with a narcissistic ex-partner whose negative impact had deeply affected her self-worth. As we addressed her nutritional requirements, we also worked through these emotional obstacles, guiding Lori to comprehend and heal from her past. This process empowered her to break free from the cycle of emotional eating.

As Lori changed her eating and exercise routines, she also transformed her internal dialogue. She began to appreciate her body not only for its appearance but also for its capabilities. Each pound lost marked a milestone in her healing journey, benefiting her physical, emotional, and mental well-being. By the program's conclusion, Lori wasn't just prepared for her daughter's wedding; she was ready to embark on a new life chapter. Equipped with newfound tools and self-love, she was poised to maintain her health and happiness long term.

**Lori George**
2 reviews

★ ★ ★ ★ ★  5 months ago

Whitney's Whole and Happy Living, Whole Health Transformation program was just what I needed to get my mindset right and my health back on track. Whitney does a great job of coaching and putting the focus on you. I needed to lose weight as I was borderline HBP and at risk for Type 2 Diabetes. She helps you make yourself a priority and helps you to dig deep into your "why". I'm thankful for Whitney and glad I made the decision to commit to doing this program for myself.

Angie's story is another powerful example of how mental and physical health are intertwined. As a working mom balancing her career and family, Angie was caught in a cycle of yo-yo dieting, her eating habits reflecting her emotional challenges. During our program, Angie discovered that her food struggles stemmed from childhood experiences and her parents' divorce. Food had become a source of comfort and security for her, a pattern she carried into adulthood.

Armed with this insight, our approach with Angie went beyond altering her diet; it centered on reshaping her relationship with food. Rather than rigid meal plans, we prioritized educating her on making nutritious choices that suited her body's requirements. Crucially, we tackled the emotional narratives linking her self-worth to her weight. Angie's transformation was comprehensive—she not only shed pounds but also developed a resilient self-esteem that positively influenced every facet of her life.

**Angie Neeley**
1 review
★★★★★  9 months ago

I absolutely loved this program!! It's much more than telling you what to eat or when to eat it. This program dives deep into why we have issues with food. I've tried almost every diet known to man and always reverted back to my old eating habits. After finishing this program, I can say I actually have a healthy relationship with food. It's been a complete lifestyle change. Whitney is awesome to work with!! I highly recommend spending the extra money on this program. You won't ever need another one again.

June's story adds a poignant dimension to our conversation. Struggling with the loss of her grandchild, June experienced profound grief that triggered a health crisis. Her diabetes, previously well-managed, became unmanageable amidst her emotional turmoil. June's journey with us focused less on weight loss and more on reclaiming control over her health and emotions. Our program equipped her with strategies to navigate grief and manage her medical condition sensitively. Her progress underscored the resilience gained from confronting deep emotional pain with empathy and guidance.

**MJune Harrison**
8 reviews · 1 photo
★ ★ ★ ★ ★  9 months ago

I have been on a personal journey of mental health for a few years now, but after the loss of my four month, old granddaughter, I knew I needed more. I saw Whitney on IG and her Whole and Happy Living program and decided to enroll.  It's been very rewarding and healing for me. to know Whitney designs the course around your needs, so that your successful. And that's absolutely wonderful, because it's at your own pace and what's best for you. No, relieving the past is never easy,  but you will definitely see progress if you keep at it!! I'm so happy that I decided to be a part of her program!!! And, McKenzie is an extra bonus! This program was definitely worth it! Thanks Whitney for putting up with me, God definitely led me to the right person ! 👍 👍 👍 👍 🖤 🖤 🖤 🖤 🖤 🖤 🖤 🖤

Cindy and Joyce's stories highlight the diverse challenges women encounter and the transformative impact of addressing them comprehensively. Cindy, grappling with stress in a demanding educational setting, learned to establish boundaries and prioritize her well-being. This shift led her to leave her job and find a new position that valued both her health and professional skills. Joyce, an entrepreneur who had always prioritized others, realized the power of self-care. By prioritizing her own well-being, she not only transformed her health but also saw positive changes in her business's success.

**Cynthia Weathers**
2 reviews
★ ★ ★ ★ ★  10 months ago

Whitney is amazing and encouraging! She is helping my mindset be different and not restrictive with foods. I love the structure of her plan! It's a real life thing...it's not a diet. Its something I will do for the rest of my life. Makenzie is also great! She has developed personalized workout plans that are doable and realistic. I am so happy to be a part of this program! I encourage anyone to talk to Whitney to see if it's the right fit for you too. Her program is exactly what I had been looking for!!

**Joyce Barton**
8 reviews
★ ★ ★ ★ ★  7 months ago

The Whole & Happy Living program is absolutely amazing!! Whitney helps so much overcome challenges that you face and helps build sustainability.  I started the end of August and with the help of Whitney and the program with the emotional and mental homework helps you learn with the help of nutrition and workout program.  I have had some challenges on the way and it is easy to getvright back up and get back on track.  I have had on and off again luck with my health journey and this program has helped my mindset of my health journey so much.  If you are looking for a program that works, this is a great program to do.  I wish I could give it more than 5 stars.

These stories go beyond mere success tales; they serve as a compelling reminder to all women to prioritize not only their diet and exercise but also their emotional and mental well-being. They highlight the core philosophy of our program: genuine health is holistic and enduring only when it's based on self-love and thorough self-care.

As we conclude this chapter, we celebrate not only the physical health improvements these women accomplished but also the profound emotional and mental breakthroughs they experienced. These stories affirm the program's fundamental principle: when you nurture your mind and spirit, your body will naturally follow suit. Let these inspiring journeys motivate you to embark on your own path towards a healthier, happier you. Remember, sustainable health is achieved through self-love and holistic self-care.

If you're ready to embark on a journey to transform your health from the inside out, we invite you to learn more about our program and schedule a call with our team.

https://www.mywholeandhappylife.com/

# KEEPING THE GAME ALIVE

Now that you've embraced the insights and strategies from Self-Love for Women, you have the power to catalyze change not just in your life, but in others' lives as well. It's time to share your newfound wisdom and guide fellow readers to the same transformative experience.

By simply leaving your honest review of this book on Amazon, you illuminate the path for other women seeking guidance on self-love and empowerment. Your opinion not only helps others discover this valuable resource but also propels the message of self-acceptance and personal growth.

Thank you for your invaluable contribution. The journey of self-love thrives when we share our discoveries—and your review helps keep this vital conversation alive.

Click here or scan the QR code to leave your review on Amazon.

Together, we continue to support and inspire one another. Your support is crucial in spreading the word and empowering more individuals to embark on their journey of self-love. Thank you for being a pivotal part of this movement.

With sincere thanks,

Whitney Prude

# CONCLUSION

*"To thine own self be true."*
– William Shakespeare

As we conclude this journey together, let's reflect on the paths we've walked—from building a foundation of self-love and embracing our vulnerabilities to setting boundaries that honor our true selves, cultivating nourishing relationships, and facing external challenges with strength. Remember, self-love isn't just about self-care; it's a deep commitment to nurturing your mental, emotional, and physical well-being.

The transformative impact of self-love is profound. By embracing it, you don't just undergo internal change; you start engaging with the world in a healthier, more positive manner. Your relationships strengthen, your mind becomes clearer, and your body benefits. It's a holistic metamorphosis that positively impacts every aspect of your life, enhancing your overall well-being.

Throughout our discussions, we've emphasized that self-love is deeply personal and not a one-size-fits-all concept. It's essential to customize the practices and principles we've explored to suit your individual life story. What resonates deeply with one person may not necessarily resonate with another, and that's perfectly normal. Remember, this journey is yours alone—distinctive and as unique as you are.

I encourage you to see self-love as an ongoing journey rather than a destination. It's a lifelong commitment that will change and evolve, much like the ebb and flow of the ocean tides. As you grow and develop, your needs and methods of self-love will also evolve. Continually revisit and adjust these practices, ensuring they resonate with your present self and circumstances.

I understand firsthand how challenging this journey can be. There were moments when I felt like retreating, wanting to escape from the emotional work it demanded. However, through patience and allowing myself the necessary space, I found a deep sense of inner freedom. Relationships that once faced difficulties now flourish because I prioritized my internal well-being first.

If my story resonates with you, please know that you are not alone. Many of us have experienced periods of self-neglect, but today is an opportunity for a fresh commitment. Promise yourself that you will never abandon the person in the mirror. You don't need to be flawless, but pledge to never turn away from yourself again.

Remember, self-love initiates a silent yet profound transformation, originating deep within your heart. This transformation has the power to influence every facet of your life. It inspires you to embrace your authentic self, not seeking validation or praise from others, but simply because you deserve your own love and kindness more than anyone else.

Now, take a moment. Stand before a mirror, look into your own eyes, and affirm:

"I will NEVER turn my back on you again!"

Embrace your journey, honor your strength, and always remember: the most powerful commitment is the one you make to yourself. Here's to a life where self-love illuminates your path!

## A Special Gift To Our Readers

Included with your purchase of this book is access to our *21-Day Habit Challenge*. This challenge will help you get started on your journey to developing healthier habits and taking better care of your body and mind in just 21 days.

Click the link below and let us know which email address to deliver it to.

https://info.mywholeandhappylife.com/habits

# REFERENCES

Prude, W. (2019, May 5). What is self-love and why is it so important? Psych Central. https://psychcentral.com/blog/imperfect/2019/05/what-is-self-love-and-why-is-it-so-important

Zemek, M. Science and self-love: Our brain and behaviour. Boxed Community. https://boxedcommunity.com/personal-development/science-and-self-love/

Breaking Taboo. (n.d.). "Self Love" in the East VS west - Articles. https://breaking-taboo.org/self-love-in-the-east-vs-west/

Quirke, M. G. (n.d.). How to nurture self-love after trauma: Rebuilding from within. https://michaelgquirke.com/how-to-nurture-self-love-after-trauma-rebuilding-from-within/

Centers for Disease Control and Prevention. (n.d.). About the CDC-Kaiser ACE study. Violence Prevention. https://www.cdc.gov/violenceprevention/aces/about.html

Holland, K. (n.d.). Cognitive restructuring: Techniques and examples. Healthline. https://www.healthline.com/health/cognitive-restructuring

American Psychological Association. (2017, January). Forgiveness can improve mental and physical health. APA. https://www.apa.org/monitor/2017/01/ce-corner

Happier Human. (n.d.). 7 Steps to effectively reparent yourself. https://www.happierhuman.com/reparent-yourself/

GoodTherapy. (2019, October 22). 11 Tips for a morning routine that supports mental health. https://www.goodtherapy.org/blog/11-tips-for-a-morning-routine-that-supports-mental-health-1022197

Tarver, J. (n.d.). 100 Journal prompts for self-discovery [+ free PDF]. https://www.jordantarver.com/journal-prompts-for-self-discovery

NIH News in Health. (2021, June). Mindfulness for your health. https://newsinhealth.nih.gov/2021/06/mindfulness-your-health

Wondermind. (n.d.). How to make positive affirmations that actually work for you. https://www.wondermind.com/article/positive-affirmations/

Leonhardt, M. (n.d.). How to overcome perfectionism: 15 Worksheets &... Positive Psychology. https://positivepsychology.com/how-to-overcome-perfectionism/

Bustle. (n.d.). 9 Social media campaigns that are changing fashion. https://www.bustle.com/articles/75539-9-body-positive-social-media-campaigns-that-are-changing-how-we-perceive-beauty-both-in-and

BetterUp. (n.d.). How to set realistic goals: 11 Tips to reach the clouds. https://www.betterup.com/blog/how-to-set-realistic-goals

HelpGuide. (n.d.). Setting healthy boundaries in relationships. https://www.helpguide.org/articles/relationships-communication/setting-healthy-boundaries-in-relationships.htm

Charlie Health. (n.d.). How toxic relationships affect your mental health. https://www.charliehealth.com/post/how-toxic-relationships-affect-your-mental-health

Harvard Business Review. (2013, February). Nine practices to help you say no. https://hbr.org/2013/02/nine-practices-to-help-you-say

WellDoing. (n.d.). How to be assertive and set healthy boundaries. https://welldoing.org/article/how-be-assertive-set-healthy-boundaries

BetterUp. (n.d.). What self-love truly means and ways to cultivate it. https://www.betterup.com/blog/self-love

Girl Power Talk. (n.d.). Transforming pain and heartbreak into advocacy: Geetha Balagopal. https://girlpowertalk.com/people-we-admire/geetha-balagopal-transforming-pain-into-advocacy/

Calm. (n.d.). 9 tips for setting healthy boundaries — Calm Blog. https://www.calm.com/blog/9-tips-for-setting-healthy-boundaries

PMC. (n.d.). Spirituality and mental health. https://www.ncbi.nlm.nih.gov/pmc/articles/PMC2755140/

The Decision Lab. (n.d.). Self-esteem. https://thedecisionlab.com/reference-guide/philosophy/self-esteem#:~:text=Together%20with%20anxiety%2C%20self%2Desteem,that%20a%20favorable%20outcome%20materializes.

Milanote. (n.d.). How to make a vision board: 2024 step-by-step guide. https://milanote.com/guide/vision-board

Benchmark Wealth Management. (n.d.). How to practice financial self-care (And why it matters). https://benchmarkwealthmgmt.com/how-to-practice-financial-self-care-and-why-it-matters/

Positive Psychology. (n.d.). 13 most popular gratitude exercises & activities. https://positivepsychology.com/gratitude-exercises/

Made in the USA
Las Vegas, NV
18 October 2024